For Steve and Sam, my two Stout men

"Life shrinks or expands according to one's courage."

—Anaïs Nin

CONTENT

ABOUT THE AUTHOR

DARCY WAKEFIELD received an MFA in Writing from Emerson College and taught English at Southern Maine Community College. Upon receiving her ALS diagnosis in 2003, Darcy and her friends and family formed Girls Kick ALS, a nonprofit organization dedicated to fundraising for ALS services and research. She lived with her true love, Dr. Steve Stout, and their baby Sam, in Cape Elizabeth, Maine, until her passing in December 2005.

I Remember Running

The Year I Got Everything I Ever Wanted—and ALS

Darcy Wakefield

MARLOWE & COMPANY

NEW YORK

I Remember Running:
The Year I Got Everything I Ever Wanted—and ALS

Copyright © 2006 Darcy Wakefield

Published by
Marlowe & Company
An Imprint of Avalon Publishing Group, Incorporated
245 West 17th Street · 11th floor
New York, NY 10011

AVALON
publishing group, incorporated

This memoir is product of the author's recollections and is thus rendered as a subjective accounting of events that occurred in her life.

Library of Congress Cataloging-in-Publication Data is available.

ISBN-10: 1-56924-279-8
ISBN-13: 978-1-56924-279-7

Book design by Maria E. Torres

ACKNOWLEDGMENTS
April 2005

I am blessed with so many fabulous friends and family that it is hard to know where—or how!—to even begin thanking them.

There's Charlotte Albright, who aired many of these essays on Maine Public Radio, and taught me to write descriptively and concisely. She also found a home for "Running" at NPR—and I will forever be in her debt for that. And speaking of NPR, I thank Sara Sarasohn for working so patiently with me to record "Running."

Many astute readers read drafts or chapters of this book and gave me invaluable help. Monica Wood and Jan Waldron provided me with thorough, helpful, and immediate feedback on the manuscript. Beth Liebson Hawkins has consistently provided sound editing and advice.

I have been unbelievably lucky to be in an outstanding writers' group. M. L. Hannay, Claudia Goldstein, Carrie Sherman, Cathy Wolff, Merrill Black, and Jan Waldron have edited, critiqued, and sometimes even typed these chapters for me. It is doubtful this book would exist if not for their help, advice, and encouragement.

In addition to the support of other writers, I count myself extremely fortunate to have the support of my dear friends, former students, and colleagues. In particular, the folks at SMCC and the UMF Upward Bound have stood with me through the hard months of diagnosis. It's hard to imagine a better group of colleagues and friends.

I am also fortunate to be associated with the Maine ALS support group; thanks to those brave, kind, and fun people who have continuously offered me hope. I also owe a big fat huge thank you to Caroline Gardiner and Dave Brook, who changed my perspective on life with ALS.

Thanks, too, to the dedicated and talented Girls Kick ALS team: Emma Holder, Amy Wood, Eileen Dugan, Dave Merrill, Michaela Cavallaro, Sarah Campbell, Betsy Wakefield, Darren Cook, Colleen Tucker, Lorraine Glowczak, Toni Parise, Lisa Wolff, and Leanne Krudner. GKALS sustained me and gave me hope on hard days— and I was continuously reminded of how blessed I was to have such unbelievable friends.

My grandmother used to have a card by her phone that read, "Friends are the family we choose for ourselves." To that end, thanks to the family I've chosen: the Beldens; the Glowzacks; the Ross family; Lisa Petruccelli; Amy Wood; Dave Merrill and Emma Holder; Sarah Campbell and Turner Kruysman; Eileen Dugan; Michael

Labriola and Jayson Hunt; and Colleen Tucker and Bill Weinschenk.

Thanks, too, to Susan Raihofer. Susan's enthusiasm, patience, and advice continue to amaze me; her astute editing and perseverance brought this book into the world.

I also would like to thank Matthew Lore, Vince Kunkemueller, Peter Jacoby, and especially Sue McCloskey for caring about my book and for all their work making a book out of my manuscript.

I'm at a loss as to how to express my gratitude to the Wakefield, Stout, and Gammon families. The support, help, and encouragement they've offered is unbelievable. I owe my mother, Nancy, and my sister Betsy a huge debt for the sacrifices they—and the rest of my family—have made to make my life more comfortable: I don't know what I would do without them.

I also don't know what I would do without Sam Stout, who is six and a half months old and sitting beside me humming as I write this; it is hard to believe that someone so young and so small could claim so much of my heart, but he has. This book is my lullaby to him.

Last of all, I owe truckloads full of thank you's to Dr. Steve Stout, who came into my life in late May 2003, a surprise and unexpected and perfect gift. I cannot imagine my life without him—but I can imagine many, many more years with him.

FOREWORD

By Jonathan Eig

I've worshiped my fair share of heroes through the years, and I'm not the least bit ashamed to admit it. After reading this book, I've added Darcy Wakefield's name to my list.

I was about four years old when Batman emerged as my first hero. He had no special powers as best I could tell—no X-ray vision, no ESP, no lightning speed—and I suspect that I was attracted to him for his relative normalcy. He was human, he improvised his responses to trouble, and he always had just the right tools in his belt, like my father. I owned a six-foot-tall wooden cutout of Batman, which I lugged everywhere for a few years, until one day I turned the caped crusader into a bicycle ramp and caused his permanent collapse.

By that time, though, it didn't matter. I had begun to shift my attention toward baseball players as heroes. I went to my local library and borrowed books on all of the game's greatest legends, and I was stirred by the stories of

Babe Ruth, Lou Gehrig, Ted Williams, and Stan Musial.
These men, too, were mere mortals. They hit baseballs
and ran the bases the same as I did, yet they were so much
bigger than life. To read these books was to immerse one-
self in a simple world of clearly defined identities: If you
hit the ball hard and won games and played fair and
showed heart, then you were a hero. There was no room
for subtlety here. Personalities made little difference.
Even in their most mundane moments, these tales of gal-
lant men were never less than breathtaking.

"He plays handball and swims in the winter months to
keep his trim 6'-0", 185-pound figure, and reports to the
Braves' spring training camp in better condition than
most of his younger teammates," wrote one of Hank
Aaron's biographers, in a passage typical of the genre.

This stuff worked its magic on me for a time. By the
time I reached the age of twelve or so, however, I had met
a couple of big-league ballplayers. Ron Blomberg had
come to my summer camp and posed for pictures with
the campers, and Dave Kingman had showed up at the
Ford dealership near my house to sign 8 × 10 glossies for
a long line of kids, and Willie Mays had appeared so fre-
quently at local walk-a-thons and Little League banquets
that I almost began to take his presence for granted. It
was about this time that it dawned on me these men were
paid for their time, and suddenly my heroes began to
seem a little too human.

I lost something with that realization. But we've all lost something with the passing of the years. Heroes are harder to come by now. Sports stars are forced to talk too much, to appear on television too often, and the more we hear and see them, the more humdrum they seem. With Hollywood stars, it's worse. The more they insist on playing parts they're not cut out for—as political commentators, for example—the dumber most of them look and sound. And let's not even talk about political commentators and politicians. Finding heroes in Washington these days is as difficult as finding the truth.

But that's not to say I've given up. In some ways, I long for heroes more than ever. That's one reason I was nervous when I began writing a biography of Lou Gehrig a few years ago. He was one of the few ballplayers I could think of (Jackie Robinson being another) who seemed to qualify in every way for hero status. Gehrig had overcome long odds to make it to the big leagues, same as his peers. But his challenges proved far greater than the rest. At the age of thirty-five, when he had good reason to look forward to several years more of productivity as the Yankees' starting first baseman and many years more of happy marriage, Gehrig learned that he had amyotrophic lateral sclerosis, a progressive and fatal neurological disease. Suddenly, baseball's strongest and most indestructible athlete was hit with an illness that lays low its victims by sapping them of their muscles.

Gehrig, while surely an ambitious man, had never cared much for celebrity. I had the impression that he would have been perfectly content to play before a stadium full of empty seats, so long as he gave it his all and helped his team to victory. Yet he was forced to respond publicly to his illness, and it was his incredibly elegant response that made him a greater figure than ever before. Only July 4, 1939, he stood before a crowd of 61,000 people at Yankee Stadium and described himself "the luckiest man on the face of the earth." Suddenly, baseball's finest first baseman was also the game's most tragic hero. He was a study in courage, a reminder that even life's most awful breaks didn't have to be crushing blows.

In the Gehrig legend, and also in the movie, *Pride of the Yankees*, the story always ended with his famous speech. His voice echoed through Yankee Stadium and he slowly stepped from the field into the shade of the dugout tunnel. Cue the violins, roll the credits. When I began researching his life, however, I knew that I would have to tell what happened next in order to make Gehrig's story complete. And this is where I put Gehrig's heroism to the test.

In the last two years of his life, Gehrig gave up his Yankee pinstripes and his celebrity. He dropped by the ballpark to see his old teammates from time to time, but he did so without calling attention to himself. He sought to live quietly but also fully. He attended operas and ballets with his wife. Not content to pass his time on a fishing boat, he took a job as a parole commissioner with the city of New York, and he reported to work every morning, right on time. But a big part of his retirement was spent in the role of ALS patient. In letters to his doctor, he maintained the same optimism he had put on display for his fans with his famous speech. He tried every treatment his doctors recommended, and when each one failed him, he urged his doctors not to give up. After all, he said, the cures might work for someone else. He maintained his sense of humor. He helped arrange theater tickets for his doctors and their families. He asked for medical advice on behalf of friends and family suffering from the most middling maladies.

That's not to say Gehrig wasn't desperate for a cure. He wanted to live, and he wanted to try everything that might give him a chance. But facing death, he chose to get on with his life.

Gehrig was just shy of his thirty-fifth birthday when he learned he had ALS. Darcy Wakefield was thirty-three. She responded to the news of the bad break with much the same grace and courage as the man for whom the disease is now named. Like Gehrig, she chose not to let the disease define her life. She decided to press forward, to make plans. In her case, that meant quitting her job, finding the man of her dreams, buying a house, getting pregnant, and giving birth to a son, all in less than a year. For a woman in perfect health, that would qualify as one heck of a year. For a woman with ALS, it's nothing short of mind boggling.

But Darcy did one more thing. She found the time and energy to write this book, coaxing her fingers along as they grew more resistant. She tells her story with eloquence, humor and honesty—and not a trace of self-pity. If anything, she feels sorry for the able-bodied woman she used to be, the one who failed to appreciate the daily wonder of being able to button one's own blouse and tie one's own shoes and walk without a hitch.

In one typically witty passage, she decides that ALS should no longer be referred to as Lou Gehrig's disease. It would be much more encouraging for modern ALS patients, she goes on to say, if the disease were named for someone who was living with the disease—someone like Darcy Wakefield, for example.

"I can't imagine ol' Lou would be too upset by this," she writes. "I'm sure he'd rather be remembered for his baseball career."

It's a generous offer. But Darcy doesn't deserve to have her name connected with this disease any more than Lou does. The illness has shaped her life, but it will never identify her. It has weakened her body, but it has helped her recognize how much strength she really possessed.

She writes that "sometimes you need to be handed a challenge bigger than anything you could have imagined in order to see the goodness in every day, in the small things. . . ."

Her life and her story remind us to embrace all of life's possibilities. That makes her a true hero.

Jonathan Eig, author of the *New York Times* bestseller *Luckiest Man: The Life and Death of Lou Gehrig,* is a senior special reporter for *The Wall Street Journal.* He lives in Chicago.

INTRODUCTION

On October 14, 2003, at St. Elizabeth's Hospital in Brookline, Massachusetts, I was clinically diagnosed with ALS (amyotrophic lateral sclerosis). Until the previous May, if asked to describe myself, I would have said that I was a single, thirty-three, athletic, active, workaholic English professor, a vegetarian who'd never had a serious health problem or injury in her life. I would have said that lately I'd been having a hard time running, but that it was probably some sort of muscle problem, nothing serious. Back then, I didn't even know what ALS was.

This book begins during that spring of 2003, when I first started having problems running, and explores the year that followed, a year in which I struggled to make sense of my diagnosis and to redefine myself. And redefine myself I did. It is impossible not to take a thorough personal inventory when your life changes so radically, so suddenly.

Once, in an e-mail to me after my diagnosis, a friend sent me this quote from *Letters to a Young Poet* by Rainer

Maria Rilke: "Be patient toward all that is unsolved in your heart and try to love the questions themselves." The quote continues, "Do not now seek the answers, which cannot be given you because you would not be able to live them. And the point is, to live everything. Live the questions now." That quote could very well be the bumper sticker of my life since October 2003. Before my diagnosis, I assumed that if I flossed my teeth, ate healthily, worked out, and didn't smoke, I'd live into my eighties, like both of my grandmothers. Being diagnosed with a terminal illness has taught me that things aren't that simple. I've quickly learned that I don't know all the answers. Indeed, I am just finding out what the questions are—questions such as, How does one accept the sudden inevitability of death, yet still live fully? What does my experience have to say about living life, even with a terminal illness?

When I was a teacher, I often assigned a free-writing activity to my students that began, "And things were never the same again." I've thought often about that exercise in the days, weeks, and months since the fall of 2003, from which time things in my life were never the same again. I've lost a lot since then—running, teaching, my identity as a healthy woman—but I've gained a lot, too. I've learned to like asking the questions, and I've learned lessons I might never have learned if I didn't have ALS.

For starters, I'm discovering that although I would

much prefer not to have ALS, things aren't as grim as they looked back on October 14 under the fluorescent lights in the small conference room at St. Elizabeth's. Living life with a death sentence, I'm learning, doesn't mean dying.

I'm also learning that sometimes you need to be handed a challenge bigger than anything you could have imagined in order to see the goodness in every day, in the small things, and in order to discover the huge, endless reservoir of courage within yourself, just waiting to be tapped, just waiting for you to dip in and draw from it.

Chapter One

BEARING [FRUIT]
February–May 2003

M ere days before Valentine's Day, my boyfriend and I broke up. On the phone.

"I'm worried about what kind of mother you'd be to the girls," he said by way of explanation as our cell phones exchanged static. It was his night with his daughters, and they were fast asleep in their upstairs bedroom. Downstairs their father—I'll call him Henry—folded laundry while we closed out our relationship.

As he talked, I thought about his girls. I hadn't met them yet; Henry was nervous about introducing new people to his young children. So the two nights a week he had the girls, I stayed clear, save for phone calls or dropping off, after they were asleep, the milk he'd forgotten to buy and wanted for their breakfast.

I'd seen their pictures, however, and had inferred a lot about them thanks to Henry's stories. He doted on them, and they seemed like nice, smart, well-mannered little girls, the type of girls who wore matching dresses and posed for pictures with their mother, also in a matching dress. I'd been eager to meet them, but, truth be told, I wasn't sure how we'd get along. Their bedroom at Henry's was always clean and they always looked clean, even in the impromptu shots on Henry's fridge. I tend to like—and get along well with—active, happy, dirty kids, kids who have manners but who also know that mud puddles are for jumping in.

In the days that followed the breakup, I kept thinking about what Henry had said to me. Finally, I took a poll of all my friends who had children. The verdict? I'd be a great mother, and they were all happy that Henry was history.

"He said *that* to *you*?" a friend and fellow teacher asked, incredulous, when I told her about Henry's comment. "Why, those girls would be friggin' *lucky* to have you as a stepmother!"

The more my friends talked, the more I realized that I'd been silly to let the relationship last as long as it had. I thought about how clear and up front I'd been with Henry about how much I wanted kids, and how he nevertheless hadn't told me about his vasectomy until well into our relationship. I was thirty-three and not getting any younger, I reminded myself. There was no point in wasting time on Henrys, wasting time mourning Henrys, or wasting time waiting around for a significant other, when my eggs were getting significantly older. A relationship I could have any time. A child, though—that had a time limit. I most certainly did not want to keep waiting for something that might not happen (a relationship) when one of the things I desperately wanted (children) was within my reach.

So I looked at my options. Adoption was too expensive on my teacher's salary, unless I wanted a high-risk or older child. Artificial insemination (AI), by contrast, looked pretty good. Except for the actual pregnancy, there were not a lot of drawbacks: there were no long forms or intensive screening processes; I could afford a few shipments of frozen sperm; and my insurance would cover the other pregnancy-related costs. I liked the idea of AI because the guys had been tested and because I wouldn't have to share parenting with someone I didn't see eye to eye with. However, it killed me to think of paying for sperm, and it did seem rather cold, getting sperm from a faceless, nameless source; it'd be nicer if I could find some friendly, free sperm.

So one night I asked another ex if he wanted to help me out. He was gentle but clear: no way. So the sperm bank it would be, and after studying the donor catalog, I fell in love with #2706. My doctor approved of him, and we made a plan: I'd reserve vials for July and August, and we'd start the AI that summer, the summer I was thirty-three.

As February turned into March, March turned into April, then April into May, I obsessed about my decision. The weather got warmer and warmer, and I tried to get back into shape after a slothful winter. *Maybe Henry was right,* I'd think as I ran. *Maybe I would be a horrid mother.* Then I'd spend some time with a young child, yearn to have one of my own, remember the poll I took of my friends, and tell myself I would find a way to make single motherhood work for me. Then I'd think about budgeting and day care and tell myself I was nuts to even consider AI.

One day when I was going back and forth like this, I caught sight of a sign at a local church. "Reflect God's love," it read, "and bear fruit."

It was just the answer I had been waiting for.

*   *   *

One day between the breakup of the relationship and the start of AI, the toaster Henry had given me for Christmas broke. When I called the company's toll-free customer service line, I explained the situation to the kind lady who took my call; my boyfriend gave me the toaster, I said, and now the toaster was like the relationship: kaput, useless, and not working for me.

"Don't worry," she said. "We'll either fix it or send you something better."

I couldn't help myself; I read into her comment, just like I'd read into the church's sign. I'm a firm believer in setting your affairs in order, making plans to do what you want, and then trusting that it will all work out. Thinking about the AI, I figured I'd done everything I could do on my end: the sperm was reserved, the doctor was chosen, my temperature was charted, and my body, according to my doctor, was healthy. Good things—no, *something better*, just as the lady had promised—were bound to come my way.

Chapter Two

DATING
June–August 2003

I've never had much luck with dating services. I tried using personal ads twice (bad idea) and a local dating service once (another bad idea), so I'm not sure why, in early March, I registered with a chichi dating service. Maybe it was because I saw it advertised in *The New Yorker.* Maybe it was because I was stinging from the Henry Situation and eager to cleanse that bad memory from my mind with a good date or two.

In any case, my naïveté was short-lived. One guy sent me an e-mail full of errors—so many that I considered contacting the Ivy League college he'd attended and turning him in. Two others were looking for pen pals. And when the only guy I agreed to go out with spent much of our date explaining why he'd named his sailboat *Mr. Hanky*, I knew my days with the service were numbered. I would simply let my membership peter out.

Besides, I was in love with Sperm Bank Donor #2706. Although he was younger than I by thirteen years, he was smart, attractive, funny, goal-oriented, and healthy. He had blond hair and blue eyes, and was into learning, reading, and writing. He would never bore me with monologues about *Mr. Hanky*. He would not write me tedious e-mails full of spelling mistakes. And he was available—or, rather, his sperm was. Looking over his profile, I couldn't help but be grateful that I'd gone ahead with Operation Baby instead of Waiting for a Relationship. Clearly, I told myself, I'd made the right choice.

The sperm bank was the best dating service I'd ever used.

* * *

Not long after, a funny, friendly, and well-written e-mail appeared in my inbox. A guy named Steve had seen my profile on the dating service Web site, and wondered if I was interested in corresponding. I skimmed his attached profile; like me, he liked the outdoors, running, hiking, and being active. I clicked open the link to his picture. He was cute. Looked energetic. Kind. I smiled at my computer, at him, and said I'd love to correspond. I didn't have high expectations. After all, Steve lived in Denver, 2,092 miles away from my Maine home.

However, we wrote constantly through June, and I was surprised at how lovely our courtship was, full of long, thoughtful, intimate e-mails. His words leaped off the screen and into my heart.

My head, however, was busy debating. Should I tell him about #2706? Or just keep mum? I didn't want to ruin our correspondence, but I knew that if I were he, I'd want to know before the relationship progressed much further. Finally I wrote him and then avoided my e-mail for as long as I could, anxious about what he'd say.

His reply surprised me. He, too, wanted kids, he wrote, and unlike me, he'd been told he wasn't a good candidate for AI. Would I do him a favor? Could we meet before the deadline? He'd buy me a ticket and I could fly out for a weekend.

It's possible, he wrote, that we could each think the other was a dork, and that'd settle things. Or maybe, he wrote, just maybe, we'd fall in love.

* * *

My excitement over Steve and my AI fixation kept my mind busy during much of June, but not so busy that I didn't have time to worry about my right foot and leg. I'd stopped running in early May because my right leg felt tight. It was hard to walk, let alone run; I could barely walk the quarter of a mile to work. By the time I reached my office, my foot would be dragging. And it seemed like I was tripping a lot; I could barely walk across my living room without a little accident. Making my way through the airport to meet Steve, I grew increasingly frustrated at how slowly I had to walk.

I'd been dreading and looking forward to this moment for days. There was this nagging doubt in my mind about Steve: he seemed too good to be true. He had no ex-wife, no kids, and no painful divorce lurking in his past. What's more, he seemed sincerely interested in what I had to say and asked questions. I was already wowed by his gentle self-confidence, sense of humor, and graciousness; besides handling the AI discussion with ease, he'd also sidestepped the stressed-out letter I'd sent him days ago, telling him—in my crankiest, most cynical New-England-confirmed-spinster voice—that we needed to be careful, that I feared we were both pinning too many of our own dreams on this meeting. Steve addressed my concerns, and then added, "Don't worry, we'll have a good time, no matter what happens."

I was still awfully nervous.

Finally I reached the baggage claim, where Steve was waiting for me. We hugged, he picked up my suitcase, and I limped to his car. Settling into the front seat, I thought briefly of the phone number in my purse: a friend's sister-in-law, whom I was to call if this Steve character turned out to be sketchy.

I never called. After Steve made me dinner, we sat on his plaid couch, sipped wine, and picked up where our e-mails had left off. Then his hand reached across cushions, states, e-mails, fears, deadlines, and doubts, until it touched mine.

* * *

There's a bumper sticker that says, "Life is what happens when you're making other plans." That's all wrong. Life, I'm learning, is what happens because you make other plans. You decide what you want and put a deposit on #2706; then suddenly Steve appears.

The second evening of my first-ever visit with Steve, after a day spent hiking, we called the airline and moved my departure date back. After all, when you find out what the "something better" is, there's no point in hurrying back home.

Chapter Three

DIAGNOSING

September–October 2003

I think it's fair to say that I have always been a good girl. I'm fairly patient, not too pushy, and careful not to create problems. But if I ever have a daughter, I want to teach her to speak up, to not be careful all the time, to take charge, and to take risks. I now regret the things I didn't say or do, the confrontations I never had, and all the times that I wasn't a better advocate for myself.

All this by way of saying that I wish I hadn't always been such a good girl.

Take, for example, the summer of 2003, when I yearned to work out. Here in Maine, there aren't a lot of good outdoor months, as far as I'm concerned. I tend to go into hibernation in late November and stay that way until late March. April through early November, I run, hike, bike, and swim.

But that summer, as May, then June, then July, and then half of August passed in a blur of nice weather, I didn't do any of those things. I was doing the Dance of No Diagnosis. I saw my primary care doc, who sent me to an orthopedic surgeon, who sent me to a physical therapist. It was the PT guy who said that I had a dropping foot, and he told me that since everything is connected, I should take it easy until he fixed what was wrong. Thus: no swimming, no running, and no hiking.

I tried, all summer, to heed his words, and to be patient with the orthopedic surgeon, who was convinced the problem was my knee, then my back; nothing that wouldn't heal itself in time. I didn't push. I didn't challenge. I didn't ask why they couldn't fix my otherwise healthy thirty-three-year-old body. Even as the summer slowly slipped away, I was a good girl.

* * *

I was also a lucky woman, because I had two doctors in my life who helped me get closer to a diagnosis.

Steve is a doctor—a psychiatrist—and as the summer passed, he urged me to have my friend John look at my leg and foot. I've known John since I was nineteen; he's a neurologist and, in the past, has been my medical advisor.

So one August night, just hours before I was to leave for Denver to see Steve for our third visit together, John took a quick look at my leg. It was weakness in the peroneal nerve, he said. If I stopped crossing my legs and tried not to sleep on that side, it should go away. If it didn't, he'd schedule an EMG (electromygram) in September.

It didn't go away, and on September 15, Steve and I went to John's office.

John let Steve into the exam room, for which I was grateful. EMGs are the closest thing to medicalized torture that I can think of. They stick needles in your muscles, ask you to move the muscle, and then study the response of your body on a computer screen. As John poked and tested me, I was grateful it was he who was doing the test, and not some doctor I barely knew and didn't trust. I was also grateful Steve was in the room, and I tried to be brave in front of him.

As the test progressed, John showed us how my responses looked on the screen. Yes, he concluded, it looked like I had weakness in the right leg, in the peroneal nerve.

Thank God it's nothing serious, I thought, relieved that the test was over.

"You know," Steve said, "I noticed yesterday that she was having a problem with her left leg, too. Could you test that?"

John obliged. The left leg. Then my back. It seemed to

me that his demeanor changed, got more serious, as the test continued. Suddenly he looked at the clock and told us he had to get to his next appointment. He said he'd call in a day with the results.

Later he would tell me that he would never have seen me as a patient had he known what he'd find that day.

* * *

I carried my cell phone with me everywhere the next day, waiting for John's call. When it finally came, I was on the third floor of Howe Hall at a Curriculum Committee meeting; my colleagues and I were talking about new courses and the committee's goals for the upcoming year.

I quickly left the meeting, and outside the conference room, in the hallway, I said hello.

"Can you go to your office?" John asked.

Before responding, I calculated the amount of time it would take me to get from Howe Hall, where the fire-fighting and law-enforcement programs are housed, and where my meeting was, to Hildreth Hall and my office. I'd have to walk down three flights of stairs, cross a small parking lot, and climb up to my second-floor office. What with my bum foot, that could take several minutes. Besides, my legs were so stiff from the previous day's EMG that I felt like I was walking on matchsticks, not bone and muscle.

No, I told John, but I could go to an empty classroom, where I closed the door and sat down at one of the long tables, surrounded by empty chairs. I'd taught in the classroom the previous spring, and I loved the views: one side of the classroom faced the common campus walkway; the other looked out on a large field, then beyond it, to the beach and ocean.

As John talked, I took notes on the only piece of paper I could find, a handout about fire extinguishers. John spoke clearly and carefully, and I tried to stay calm and write down the words correctly so that I could sort them out later, in my office or at home, somewhere where I could privately re-examine the phrases, such as "motor nerve degeneration" and "deintervation in muscles that are clinically normal."

"Darcy," John said, "this could be something serious." He then told me that he was making an appointment for me with a neuromuscular specialist in Boston, two hours away. "You need to be prepared to hear the words 'motor neuron syndrome' in Boston."

Motor neuron syndrome?

"ALS," John said.

Once again, I was quiet. What the hell was ALS?

"Lou Gehrig's disease."

* * *

Despite his best efforts, the earliest appointment John could get for me was October 14. One month away.

Suddenly it seemed like I was living in a blurry sort of monthlong hell. Nights I cried until the sleeping pills kicked in. Days I went to work, tried to teach, got angry at students for not doing the reading. Sometimes I remembered to eat; often I did not. Not surprisingly, by October 14, I had lost ten pounds. One hundred and sixteen pounds on a 5'8" body is not an awful lot, for the record.

Between classes, I'd sit in my office and study motor neuron diseases. I took a day off (bringing the total sick days I've used in my teaching career to 2.5) for blood work. I tried going out with friends and co-workers, but it was hard. Well-meaning people kept telling me it was probably nothing. I shared their disbelief; after all, I was thirty-three, healthy, female. ALS, I'd read, strikes mostly men, mostly older than I. But my research told me that there were not a lot of other possibilities. Finally, I asked John if it could be anything else. All he would say is that "some people live a long time with this."

* * *

As the days moved me closer to the October 14 appointment, I began to understand that I needed to advocate more for myself, at least when it came to my medical needs. I was grateful that Steve had pushed me to see John, that John had squeezed me into his schedule, that Steve had asked him to check the other leg, and that John had pushed through the appointment with the specialist and gotten my insurance's OK. I was grateful that Steve could help me navigate my way through the articles and medical terms and Web sites. I couldn't begin to imagine how differently things might have turned out had I not known John or if I weren't dating Steve.

I was angry, too, at the time I'd wasted being patient over the summer, perfectly lovely days I could have spent speed walking, hiking, swimming. I vowed that never again would I let anyone, no matter how well-intentioned they were, tell me what was best for me and my health or safety.

And as the days slowly passed, I grew increasingly more frustrated at a medical establishment that allows a patient given such horrible news to wait a month for a specialist. I wished that all insurance executives, high-ranking government officials, hospital directors, and hard-to-see doctors had to live for a month as an average person knowing that they, too, might have an incurable, fast-moving disease—and knowing there was nothing they could during that month but be patient and wait.

Chapter Four

BURNING
October 2003

I will always remember the Sunday before the Boston appointment in vivid color. The details are clear, bright, crisp, like the weather we had that day. Steve was back for another visit; he'd arrived on Friday night, Saturday we'd hung out around my apartment, and Sunday we hiked Mount Chocorua in New Hampshire. We took the back route to avoid the crowds, and once we switched off the old road and onto the trail, we were alone.

At the summit we admired the view and the fall foliage; lunched on apples, hummus, cheese, and bread; and then sprawled out for short naps in the sun. Later, on the way down the mountain, a one-legged hiker passed us. He was booking it. He seemed to me to be one more piece of this fabulous day, like the unexpectedly warm weather and the beautiful foliage and the challenging hike.

All day Steve and I spoke of leaves, mountain bikers, bugs, the sun; we didn't talk about the upcoming appointment with the neuromuscular specialist, two days away. Every time I started to worry about the diagnosis, I'd tell myself that I was being silly. After all, I wasn't even forty, and I certainly wasn't male; there was no way I could have ALS. No way at all.

* * *

Two days later, on October 14, we went to St. Elizabeth's Hospital, where I had a pulmonary test, a swallowing test, a spinal tap, and another, more comprehensive EMG. This time they wouldn't let Steve into the room—and this EMG was even worse: they tested every part of my body. I started crying with the first needle and didn't stop until the last. I was alternately glad Steve wasn't in the room— I was a mess—and angry that he wasn't allowed. It'd have been nice to hold his hand, to try to be brave for his sake.

Late afternoon, after most of the tests were over, the neuromuscular specialist asked us to join him in the conference room, and then closed the door and sat at the table with us. He knew we wanted answers, he said, and he was going to be straightforward and tell us the truth.

It was ALS.

"You've had this for some time and didn't know it," he told me. I thought of my legs; they'd grown flabby, which was highly unusual for me; I had blamed it on not running. My arms were also loose and jangly, and I thought of how difficult it'd been to lift things for the past year. I remembered how hard it had been to talk on the cell phone, to keep the phone at my ear without the right arm going weak. I looked at my hands—already caving in, as the doctor pointed out, from want of muscle. My handwriting had been getting worse over the past few months, and I had attributed it to grading so many papers and frequent computer use. Why hadn't I put it all together?

There was a 10 percent chance, the doctor told us, that the blood tests I'd do before leaving the hospital that day might show something else, but he was fairly certain my clinical diagnosis was what I'd taken to calling The Big Bad One.

It had been a long day of tests, and as I listened to the doctor, I took notes as Steve asked our questions. Later Steve would clarify stuff I hadn't gotten entirely right.

Finally we asked the doctor the question that concerned me the most. Would I be able to have a baby?

The doctor looked surprised. This question, I would soon find, was something that doctors diagnosing ALS are not in the habit of having to answer.

He didn't think it'd be a problem, but he reminded us of the toll that pregnancy takes on a woman's body. Then he told us something that would stay in my brain and continue to resonate: "There is nothing you can do to make this any worse."

* * *

The days that immediately followed were a blur, thanks to shock and a painful spinal headache, which I'd gotten minutes after the spinal tap the doctor had given me after the EMG and exam. Sometimes after a spinal tap, the spinal fluid leaks. It creates a headache unlike anything I've ever felt before—making it hard to sit up, eat, or talk. Finally, two long days after the spinal tap, a neurologist in John's practice patched up the leak with a procedure that hurt as much as the original spinal tap had. I threw up, it hurt so much. Or maybe it was a delayed reaction to all the painful tests I'd undergone in the last month. In any case, my headache stopped almost immediately, and I had room in my head to think about my life. When the new clarity washed over me, I almost wished the spinal headache back.

I soon lapsed into a state of dreamlike numbness. I often asked myself, Do I want to live or do I want to die? I struggled to find an answer. Of course I wanted to live— but did I want to live with this diagnosis? I knew that I'd rather kill myself before the ALS killed me, and I thought of ways I could do it: I asked a lawyer friend to look into euthanasia for me. I found a friend who was willing to help me overdose when I was ready to die, if I couldn't do it myself. I conducted my own Internet research to find out my options.

One day in the middle of a panic attack, I called the ALS Association, and the woman who answered the phone told me that she wasn't in the business of giving false hope. However, she said, in many cases the ALS reaches a point and burns out. Everyone's ALS progresses differently, she told me.

Later I ran across an article in an ALS publication that said something similar: that in a small number of folks, the ALS disappears. There are others whose ALS burns out, and there are some whose ALS progresses very slowly.

Not long after talking with the woman and reading the article, I went to a Denver church with Steve. In the bulletin, we were reminded that "every part of you was once inside a star."

These words resonated. I'd been feeling tingly since the September appointment, and at first figured it was the aftershock of the EMG. Then, after I knew more about ALS, I feared the tingling was my motor neurons shorting out. But after reading that line in the church bulletin, I told myself it was just the constellation inside me twinkling. I let myself hope that the sensation was the start of the ALS working its way out of me, and I imagined that the ALS was only a comet, shooting across the inside of my body; like a comet, it would burn out. Then, soon, it'd be gone.

Chapter Five

DYING
October 2003

I grew up in western Maine, where animals die. I knew people who ate the chickens, pigs, and cows they raised. Roadkill—woodchucks, cats, skunks, you name it—was not an uncommon sight, nor were the dead deer dangling out of the backs of pickup trucks, nor was the flailing mouse hanging out of my cat's mouth. Although I never grew comfortable with these sorts of animal deaths, I certainly grew accustomed to them.

One week in late September, days after my appointment with John, there were suddenly dead animals everywhere, animals who had died odd deaths. At Old Orchard Beach, I saw a woodchuck, washed up, stiff as plywood and looking sort of surprised, and two fish, their corpses picked clean. The next day, on the walkway at the college where I teach, there was a squirrel curled on its side; someone had arranged a few cigarette butts, fanlike, by his mouth. And then, one morning at Willard Beach, not far from where I live, there were the little silver fishes: some of their tiny bodies were still alive and flapping, and they made a long, thin ribbon of silver on the brown sand.

The Week of the Dead came to an end and was followed by a wicked storm. When I went down to the harbor a few days later, I saw that a sailboat had come free of its mooring, and was beached on a pile of rocks. The rocks tore the boat open like a cooked lobster. I stared at that boat skewered on the craggy rocks, high out of reach of all but the highest tide.

* * *

Not long after, the neuromuscular specialist in Boston confirmed that I had ALS, and I began doing a range of unpleasant tasks. I saw a lawyer about making a will. I named a power of attorney. I wrote a health-care directive. I spoke with John about what to expect with an ALS death. I made funeral arrangements.

For years, I've listened to my maternal grandmother talk about all things death-related: how she wants to die, who will get her house, and how relieved she is to have long-term-care insurance so she can die in her own home. It used to make me feel uncomfortable and sad. Now, though, I realize how comforting it actually is to tie up all the threads that most of us are content to leave loose.

My grandmother's ease in talking about death may have something to do with her age. At eighty-seven, she's buried a lot of people. Death is real to her. At thirty-three, my age, death is more abstract. Indeed, a funeral home director, a financial planner, and a wills and estate lawyer have all told me that it's almost impossible to get younger people to plan for death.

I don't blame them. It was hard writing a will and giving somone power of attorney; I brought my sister along. Going to the funeral home was easier, as was planning the post-funeral gathering. I tried to convince myself that I was simply planning a large party I wouldn't be able to attend, but would be able to watch on closed-circuit TV.

And then I wrote my own obituary. My funeral home would have done this for me, but as a seasoned obit reader and English teacher, there was no way I was going to let someone else write it. I know from experience that I don't work well with others writing my story: many years ago, when I joined a dating service, they wrote up a bio of me to send to potential dates. I had to give up editing their mistakes, but I hated knowing that there was a bio of myself floating around the dating service that had a comma splice in it. The same thing, I figured, held true here: I could never depart this world fully and freely if my obituary was poorly written.

I did those things—the funeral arrangements, the obit, the legal work—so that I could concentrate on living. And that's what I try hard to do, although I still occasionally think about death.

I used to think, when I ever thought about it, that suffocating would be the worst way to go. However, these days, if given a choice between suffocating or dying of ALS, I'd take option A; indeed, if I am to believe all I have read about this illness, my body will be picked clean by it, and the end won't be particularly pretty or smooth. Many accounts of ALS deaths mention the mental torture of the final months, when the patient—me—is alert, locked in a working mind, while everything else is shutting down, including the ability to speak or move. This is the worst kind of death I can imagine.

If I could choose, I would die old and in my sleep, but at this point, I'd take *anything* other than an ALS death.

I wouldn't mind dying like the little silver fishes, tossed up on shore with my fish buddies: a few last flaps, then death. I wouldn't mind going as the sailboat went: one big wind, then the quick pain of rocks to my middle, then my end. I wouldn't even mind dying like that poor squirrel— a sudden fall from a tree, a splat onto the sidewalk—just as long as prankster students stayed away from my corpse. Or I could die as the woodchuck did, washing up on a hard, smooth beach somewhere in southern Maine, whole and dead and stiff and plump and slightly surprised.

Yes. That's it. I, too, want to wash up on a hard, smooth beach somewhere in southern Maine, whole and dead and stiff and plump and slightly surprised.

Chapter Six

NAMING
October 2003

I study language the way others follow sports teams, and examine words like stats. I have spent years talking to college students about the wording of their essays and the language of the poems, essays, stories, and plays we've read. After the school day was done or before it began, I spent time at my computer, where I tinkered with language and agonized over sentences and their structure. I tune into words the way others tune into music: they hear beats and words and memorize lyrics; I hear sounds and see combinations of letters.

Not surprisingly, then, in my post-diagnosis days, I automatically turned to words for comfort. I perused medical books and ALS Web sites to learn more about my disease, I took solace in poetry, and I searched for books by people with ALS to learn from their experiences. I read piles of pamphlets that ALS organizations sent me.

And it was in the course of my reading that I learned that people with ALS sometimes lose the use of their voice and the use of their hands. To say this scared me does not come close to describing the terror I felt when I imagined not being able to use my voice or my hands. As my reading progressed and my terror subsided (a little), I began to notice the language of disease, something I had never paid much attention to. It was hard to ignore, though: in the very words I usually found comfort in or took information from, I also found a vocabulary that didn't fit the new me, a vocabulary that included words like *patient* and *disabled. I'm no patient and I'm not patient,* I'd mutter to myself every time I read or heard the phrase *ALS patient.* And the word *disabled* would trigger a tsunami of substitutions in my head: *motor neuron challenged* or *multi-abled,* I'd whisper to myself whenever anyone used the d-word in reference to me. Even the ALS community has a vocabulary that bothers me. The word *caregiver,* for instance, is commonly used to describe the people who help a person with ALS, and it diminishes the wholeness of everyone's contribution. Steve is no longer my partner, he is my *caregiver*—and I become defined by my need to be cared for.

But perhaps more significantly, I also struggle with the

name of my disease. In many countries, the illness is known as ALS or motor neuron syndrome. In the United States, however, it is also known as "Lou Gehrig's disease," and it is not uncommon to see references in papers and articles that read like this: "ALS, more commonly known as Lou Gehrig's disease . . ." It's wordy, I find; why not simply call ALS "ALS"?

Here's my main concern with calling my syndrome "Lou Gehrig's": to name this disease after a white male almost allows us to forget that ALS is an equal-opportunity illness. As a guy with ALS once said, "ALS: it's not just for baseball players anymore." Indeed, ALS knows no social, ethnic, or racial boundaries; women, even young women like me, get it.

Besides, to name ALS after someone who died from it isn't exactly encouraging or hopeful. If we are going to insist on naming ALS after a person, we need to name it after someone who is alive—like me. Therefore, I have taken the liberty of renaming it the Darcy Wakefield Anti-Disease, or DWAD. I can't imagine ol' Lou would be too upset by this; I'm sure he'd rather be remembered for his baseball career.

A few months ago, if someone had told me that I'd spend hours agonizing over the word *disabled* and the name *Lou Gehrig's disease*, I would have called them crazy. Back then, I would have said that if I ever had a terminal illness, I certainly wouldn't waste time worrying about *words.* Now, though, I'm a different woman. I often feel as if my identity has been put in a blender, and I'm finding that when you are in danger of losing your ability to quickly communicate, it becomes even more important that you are comfortable with the words others use to describe your illness, your abilities, and your self.

Chapter Seven

RUNNING
Late October 2003

I remember running. I remember running like I remember the sun-filled beach days of my childhood. I remember running like many remember their first love, their first kiss, their wedding. I remember running and feel the ache of absence, the heavy reminder that my life will never be the same again.

I am continuously mourning running.

* * *

I started running during my junior year of college. I liked running because I could do it alone or with friends, and I could do it almost anywhere, too. I'd run on vacation, exploring unfamiliar cities. At home, I'd run mornings when the weather wasn't ugly. At work, I would sprint to my classes or down the hall to the photocopier or over to the cafeteria for a snack. After work, I'd dash into the post office, or I'd run to the library. Weekends I'd chase my parents' dog, then he'd chase me, when the family took a walk. I loved running.

Last year, I ran until early November, when the oncoming Maine winter limited me. In February and March when the weather cleared for a day or two, I got in a few runs, but they were simply sweet reminders. Then, in April, the weather cleared for more days and the mud came, and I began running again. I was unusually stiff and slow, but I figured it was punishment for years of not stretching and a winter of rarely running. So I stretched and ran and stretched and iced, but it was increasingly harder to get my legs to cooperate, especially my right leg, which seemed tight and useless, and my right foot, which turned inward.

Then, on one of my morning beach runs, it felt like my right leg snapped.

Gastrocnemius, my friends and I decided. My doctor said I should stay off it and ice it for a week, which I did, but the days were getting warmer and I longed to slide my tights back on, to feel the road under my sneakers. So after a week, I tried running again. My goal was to train during the late spring and early summer for Beach to Beacon, a local road race.

Looking back now, I wish I had known these were my last runs. I would have appreciated every hill, every post-run high, every minute my legs moved in that way we call running.

* * *

Even though I no longer run, I still have a runner's soul, and it is trapped in a runner's body that won't run. My runner's soul longs to work off the stress of my diagnosis and the stress of not running with a good run. It doesn't yet understand what has happened to us.

But my mind understands, and because of this, there are days when I cannot stand to talk about running or see someone running. These moments pass, and I try to find pleasure in this new pastime of mine, being a spectator. I let myself admire other runners and fantasize that I am them. I imagine how good their feet must feel on the asphalt. I can almost feel the spandex tights on their thighs. I tell Steve to appreciate every moment, every sensation, every detail of his runs because he is running for two now.

I try, too, to take pleasure in what now substitutes for running in my life. The other night, something told me to go down to the beach, and I did, even though it was late and dark. The only sound was the clang of sailboats in the harbor. The beach was hard and smooth because the tide was out. Then something told me to run. I ran back and forth and around and around in small, then larger circles. If you had seen me, you wouldn't have called what I was doing running, but it was good enough for me. I took off my shoes, too, and let my stockinged feet part the cold sand. This is what I thought that night as I gave thanks: *We are so lucky to be able to do this, all of our nerves and muscles working together as we move ourselves forward to do this thing we call running.*

It was hard to leave the beach that night. I wanted to keep doing my loops. But finally I picked up my shoes and walked back to the car, taking comfort in the knowledge that one day, I might run again. Maybe not in this life, but definitely in the next, when I say hello to God and family and friends who've gone on before me, then look down at my feet only to realize that I have on my favorite running sneakers. Ahead of me is a beach stretching for miles and miles and miles. The tide is out, so there's a nice band of hard sand at the water's edge. It is sunny but not humid, with a slight breeze. Perfect running conditions. I pick up my feet—and run.

Chapter Eight

EATING
November 2003

I n the past few months, I've had a spinal tap, two X-
rays, two EMGs, a pulmonary test, hours of MRIs, and
a swallowing test. I've also given up one container of urine
and twenty-one tubes of blood. Not to brag or anything,
but what these tests have shown is that other than ALS,
there is nothing wrong with my body; it's in great shape.
But I already knew this. I eat vegetarian. I don't smoke. I
drink in moderation. I eat when I am hungry and I stop
when I'm full. However, I haven't always been this nice to
my body. I used to overexercise; I used to wear out my
body with work, and I used to diet and withhold food—
even when I was hungry. I stopped being so mean to my

body a few years ago, and yet I still have programmed into my psyche the desire for a perfect, thin body.

Like the other night, when I was in the bathtub. I'd just eaten a big dinner, and my stomach was full and puffed out. I looked down at it with disgust, and then caught myself. Thanks to muscle loss, I now weigh 115 pounds. Those pounds are stretched tightly over my 5'8" frame. Isn't that thin enough? Isn't that too thin? When does the desire to be thin, to be perfect, stop?

I know I'm not alone. Almost every woman I know has a stressful relationship with food or with her body. Right now a few of my dear, beautiful friends are on diets. At restaurants and parties I've watched them decline yummy desserts and avoid certain foods. Lately I've seen this behavior in male friends, too, many of whom are on the Atkins diet; they reel off a list of foods they cannot eat, followed by a list of foods they crave. They speak of pasta and pizza the way I speak of running. They talk about the last dessert they ate the way my ex-smoker friends talk about cigarettes.

When I listen to these dieting folks, it takes all the restraint I can muster not to tell them how lucky they are that their bodies are taking on weight, that they can swallow all the food they want, that they can exercise that food into muscle. I would give anything to gain some weight, to cover my ribs and knees and hands with a layer of fat to cushion the falls I'm prone to taking. I'd give anything to run those new pounds into muscle or hike them into nonexistence.

In the days following my diagnosis, one comment I heard often was, "Well, now you can eat anything you want." Another comment was, "Now you can stop flossing." My gut response to these comments was annoyance. I mean, really, we are all going to die sometime; shouldn't we all eat whatever we want? Shouldn't we all stop flossing?

Besides, and more important, I love flossing, and I already eat whatever I want. I am most certainly not going to change my eating habits now that I have ALS—unless, of course, it is to eat even more healthily and to enjoy eating even more. Someday I may no longer be able to swallow. Just before that happens, if I let them, doctors will slice into my body and insert a feeding tube. I dread this. This dread informs my appreciation for everything I swallow, everything I am lucky enough to eat, every pound that attaches itself to my body. So from now on, I'm going to like—really like—my body just as it is. No mean-spirited comments. No guilt for eating too much. No wishing for something different.

Chapter Nine

SWERVING

November 2003

She was swerving the whole way across the Casco Bay Bridge. She was driving slowly, too, really slowly in the left lane, and a few of us passed her on the right, holding our breath and waiting until she veered to the left. I don't know why I didn't just stay behind her, but it was late—9:20 PM or so—and she was slow and I was anxious to get home. *Elderly driver,* I thought, even though that's a stereotype.

As I got near the intersection, I put on my directional and pulled into the left lane. Sitting at the red light, I looked in my rearview mirror: she was coming up behind me. But she slowed, and seemed to come to a stop way over to the side of my car, as if she was thinking about maybe taking a right turn, but stopped nonetheless. I looked back at the still-red light, then felt my neck snap back and heard the crunch of bumpers connecting.

She'd hit me.

After I put on my emergency lights and got out of my car, I saw that the driver was about my age. She kept saying something about being almost home, about five hundred more yards to go. She said she'd had three drinks, but I guessed more. I'll admit, I looked at her Saab; I took note of her healthy, drunk, warm body; and I heard her say, "My father is a lawyer." I felt righteous and angry, me in my 1992 Honda Civic, me with my recent ALS diagnosis, me sober and cold.

So I called the police. I didn't tell her, of course; I told her I was getting my insurance stuff from my car. When the officer arrived, I was standing beside her car, and she was trying to convince me to follow her to her house, to come in for coffee.

The officer told me to pull up ahead and asked me to write out my statement. It was hard—my right hand was cold from all that time outdoors chatting with Miss Saab, and it wouldn't cooperate. All day I'd been having problems with it, and I feared it was going the route of my right foot, the first limb to visibly atrophy.

As I struggled to write out the information the officer wanted, I thought about all that had happened that night, about how I could have backed down and not called the police. I could have followed her home and gone inside for coffee. Possibly she and I had a lot in common. And in the past, that's probably what I would have done, backed down, said "No problem" when Miss Saab said I should just get out of her way, just let her drive on home. But I didn't. I'd like to say I called the police because I worried that even if I let her go and she made it home safely that night, that she might drive home drunk the next and hit someone else. But really, all I could think about that night was me: What if she'd hit me harder, me with my death sentence already? What if she'd shortened my already short time?

Somehow I finished the statement and drove home, my hand on the gearshift, numb and useless, an ever-present reminder that although my life had been spared this evening, it was only for the time being.

Chapter Ten

SWIMMING
December 2003

One day in late October, not long after the Boston appointment, Steve took me to a pool not far from his Denver home. I was skeptical, I'll admit, as I put on my old orange two-piece, swim cap, and goggles. I have always disliked pools and the smell of chlorine. I'm more a lake-water kind of girl, and I've been swimming in Maine lakes since I was a kid. At the lake, there are no lanes, no structured swim hours, no plastic lane dividers, no hard-to-put-on swim caps, and no other swimmers crowded up next to me, sending water up my nose whenever I turn my head to breathe.

I thought of all this as I got into the Denver pool. There was no float at the other end of the pool, no promise of a loon sighting, no warm sunshine on my back—but as I started my laps, my skepticism dissolved into an odd sort of high. Since my diagnosis, I'd been feeling diseased, out of shape. It's hard to find ways to burn off my energy, to find substitutes for speed walking, running, hiking. But as soon as my body started doing the crawl, it all came back. My legs kicked, my arms moved, my head turned sideways. I felt my body slide through the water, just like it used to.

Since then, back home in Maine, I've taken to swimming at a pool just up the road from my house. Often it is just me, a handful of retirees, a homemaker or two, some young kids taking swim lessons, and a few people from a group home. Some of us walk to the pool, some get to the pool with walkers, others use the pool wheelchair and the long, sloping ramp. In the water we clutch kickboards, float on long noodle-like things, and do laps and aerobics. We midday swimmers are a busy bunch.

Although I miss lake swimming, I try to get to the pool as often as I can. It seems like the best option for me right now, with my unpredictable legs and the Maine winter. Surprisingly, I'm finding that the chlorine smell no longer repels me. In fact, it is an aphrodisiac; it calls to me, and I answer. As I feel my limbs go through the motions of years past, I let my body think it's healthy and whole. I let it pretend it's back in Long Pond, swimming laps between the float and the dock, the only lifeguard on duty my parents' German shepherd.

As I swim back and forth in my lane, I have time to think about all the changes in my life. I'm beginning to understand that when your world seems to narrow, you need to learn to find pleasure where you can. And if you are willing to slide into the cold water, your body will remember, and the memories will buoy you up, move you forward, make you whole. And the world will widen back out again.

Chapter Eleven

HOUSE HUNTING
December 2003

A few days after my diagnosis, a well-meaning friend told me to get on the waiting list at a good assisted-living facility. Her words scared me, and briefly I panicked: an assisted-living home? At thirty-three years old, I couldn't imagine living in a place like that. Fortunately, Steve told me that I wouldn't have to—because he was moving from Colorado, his home of nine years, to Maine, and we would live together. In a house.

A house! I had wanted a house for years. I had wanted to settle down, to put down roots in this part of Maine that I love. So when Steve started talking about houses, I fantasized along with him. We talked about good neighborhoods, the importance of sunlight, a garage, a nice kitchen. We looked at houses online, I clipped ads from the Sunday paper, and we drove around checking out open houses. All along, I found myself drawn to old New England houses with lots of windows and small staircases and creaking back stairs and tiny rooms and character and old woodwork and beat-up wood floors. I looked at these houses and imagined us in them—until one night when Steve reminded me that we needed a house with a downstairs bath and bedroom, something wheelchair accessible, at least on the first floor.

His gentle reminder marked the end of my carefree house-hunting days. Instead of looking at houses and noticing the sweet built-ins or the good sunlight or the working fireplace, I looked instead for accessible bathrooms, first-floor bedrooms, wheelchair-wide doorways, and entryways that could handle a ramp. Every house became not a happy landmark of moving in with Steve, but instead a constant reminder of my predicted disability.

This issue of accessibility is something I'm beginning to understand, fast. During the summer of 2003, back when I thought my foot/leg issue was nothing serious, I read in the local paper that the town and a private donor had chipped in to buy a special wheelchair for the local beach. I remember being surprised (I'd never heard of such a thing), and wondering who would use it. After all, I never saw disabled people at the beach.

I no longer wonder who would want to use such a thing because now I know. Through the cold of this winter, I've been grateful that the donor and the town had such fore-sight. I like knowing that there is a beach near me that almost anyone can get to, even if it's only when a lifeguard is around to fetch the chair.

My beach's accessibility, however, is unusual. And even though someone in a wheelchair could get to the local beach, they'd have a hard time getting into most homes. As Steve and I looked at houses all over southern Maine, I found myself asking the same questions, over and over: Where do the people in wheelchairs live? And who the heck do they visit? *Oh,* I would think as I climbed stairs, squeezed into bathrooms, eyed doorway width, *oh, for a world where all houses were accessible.*

We gave up trying to find an accessible home, and instead bought an adorable Cape Cod cottage that will need some renovating and possibly a ramp. For now, we're remodeling the downstairs bathroom to make it roomier, we've put the washer and dryer on the first floor, and we installed easy-to-grasp handles on two of our outside doors so that I can open and lock them by myself.

In addition to the physical changes being made to the house, I'll also need to renovate my mind by the time we move in in early February. How do I erase all the negative associations I now have with this house? How do I look at it as a place to raise a family, a place where we'll grow old, even as Steve and I talk about ramp aesthetics, turnaround space for wheelchairs, and shower handrails? How do I live in the present when I am surrounded by reminders of the future that is predicted for me?

This is what I know now: Steve is moving across the country to be with me. I know, too, that I spend too much time worrying about tomorrow, about money and wheelchairs and doctors and dying and insurance and vitamins—and I need to stop. I don't want to live life overshadowed by what might come my way. I don't want to waste time today worrying about what tomorrow might bring.

So I push all the fears and concerns aside, and focus instead on our new home, with its old windows and wood floors and funny corners and sweet built-ins and accessible first floor—and I imagine myself living in this house for a long, long time.

Chapter Twelve

HEARTBREAKING
December 2003

In the apartment above me, a baby cries, briefly, until his mother soothes him. He is four months old, and not a day passes when I don't get some reminder that there is a child just out of my reach. I've wanted children since forever, and my goal was to be pregnant by the time I turned thirty-four. In a matter of days, I will turn thirty-four. I am not pregnant. Some days it is all I can do not to wail along with the child upstairs.

* * *

If you go inside my brain for just a minute, you will interrupt the continuous prayer that runs through my head, as constant as my breathing. *Please,* I pray, *get rid of this ALS. Let it burn out, be cured, disappear. And please, let me have a healthy baby and let me see the child through to adulthood.*

Sometimes I interrupt myself to say that I have no business thinking that I should have a child. What if my disease progresses? Is it fair to ask Steve to raise a child and care for me? After all, the medical literature about ALS pregnancies is nothing short of depressing: "The long-term maternal outcome is universally dismal," was the conclusion of one article.

A friend, hearing of our struggle with this decision, says that it will be heartbreaking for me to die with a child, and I agree. However, since getting ALS, I've become familiar with the concept of heartbreak. It is heartbreaking to have ALS. Not having a child is a heartbreak that swallows me whole, surrounds me like a second skin made of hurt. Some days it comes in an anger, a burst of dismay at the unfairness of it all. Other days it is more like a hangover, ever-present and hard to get rid of. Sometimes it is a tiny pearl, lodged in my brain.

What, I wonder, is one heartbreak compared with another?

Sitting in a doctor's office one day, I was surrounded by women in all stages of mothering and their children of various ages. I tried to read a magazine, but there was no holding back the ache. It's the same ache that I feel when friends talk about their kids, when I see a young child, or when I hear that yet another woman my age has had a baby. It is an ache that starts deep in my heart and drills down into me, down into that tender spot that is scraped raw with want.

So I try to figure out in advance how to hold my grief in check, but there are always surprises, like the impromptu baptism one Sunday in church; or the friend who unexpectedly brings her child along on a coffee date; or the mail full of Christmas cards of happy, smiling babies. I weigh the unopened envelopes carefully, hold them up to the sunlight, estimate how much they'll hurt to open. Some I open quickly; some I file away for later; the rest I throw out, unopened.

* * *

The high-risk-pregnancy doctor Steve and I consult says that we should go for it, but we shouldn't dilly-dally. She tells me that I am healthier than most folks at the mall. The genetic counselor says there is a risk when anyone reproduces, not just when people like me do. The ALS material I read warns me not to take the statistics I've seen about ALS too seriously and to remember that everyone experiences ALS differently.

So after weeks of agonizing, we decide not to dilly-dally. I myself give the decision over to the universe: *There*, I say, *you decide if I should have a child.* I become hopeful—and generous, kind even, when others talk about their kids, when smiling baby pictures arrive in the mail, when the youngster upstairs cries. I am hoping that my graciousness will earn me baby points, that I may soon be a parent.

I tell my acupuncturist that we're going to try to get pregnant. She is quiet for a minute, then she says that she can work with me. She tells me that to give birth is to give up years from one's life. This is what I hear her say: *To give birth is to give up one's life.*

I tell her I'm ready.

Chapter Thirteen

COMMITTING

December 2003

S teve and I began talking about long-term commitment on Christmas Eve.

I told him he only wanted to get me into bed, but we
both know that is a lie. It doesn't take much for him to get
me into bed, and certainly not the promise of commitment.

And besides, I'm already committed to him. Being with
him seems so right, so natural, like getting up in the
morning and swinging my feet over the bed's edge and
standing up. I love him with a love that is sometimes too
big for me.

But while our commitment to each other is a no-
brainer, the issue of what sort of commitment we want to
make is a lot more loaded. Since my ALS diagnosis in

mid-October, we've wrestled with this issue. ALS is an expensive disease; what if we married and my disease ruined our finances? By contrast, if we don't legally marry, I will destroy only mine.

But if we don't legally marry, what sort of commitment can we have? For Steve, the issue is straightforward. He has always wanted to get married; he wants to be able to introduce me to people as his wife. He isn't hell-bent on a big, fancy wedding, nor does he need the legal commitment, but he does want to join a tradition that his friends and family have taken part in, something that works well for them. This is, he tells me, very important to him.

For me, the issue is a bit more complicated. I look at my dear, sweet Steve, and hate to deny him anything he wants so badly. But thanks to my diagnosis, I've got some wedding issues. For starters, if we were to marry, what would I wear? The only shoes I can walk in comfortably, without tripping, are my hiking boots and trail sneakers. I cannot imagine trying to coordinate them with a wedding gown or even a nice dress. There's also the identity issue: since October, my identity has changed radically. Not surprisingly, I'm nervous about trading in what I've been able to salvage of the old Darcy Wakefield to become A Wife.

But to be truthful, I have commitment issues that stretch back to well before my ALS diagnosis. I've always loved reading the Sunday *New York Times* wedding announcements (what I like to call my Sunday morning erotica), but have never imagined myself getting married and have always hated attending weddings—probably because when I was younger, my mom took me and my sister to a lot of wedding showers, where I was always either incredibly nauseated or covered in hives. A doctor finally diagnosed my nut allergy, but by then it was too late; I already associated showers, and therefore weddings and matrimony, with hives and heaving.

As I got older, I started carrying an EpiPen and liking weddings more. But it's still hard for me. I've come to understand and appreciate how important matrimony and wedding ceremonies are to people, and it makes me feel bad that so many committed couples are excluded from getting married. I know that gays and lesbians can have commitment ceremonies without the legal privileges, and I know, too, that many don't want to get married. But it bothers me that not all couples can choose whether or not they want to take advantage of something that has so many legal, financial, and social benefits.

Steve understands how complex the subject of matrimony is for me, and for now, we've tabled the commitment discussion. But the rest of the world hasn't caught up: for weeks people have been asking me if Steve and I are getting married.

Here's what I've considered telling people who ask: when you get a diagnosis like mine, you quickly figure out what matters to you, and how you want to spend your time. It's almost like my life was thrown up on a white wall, and what's important remained—like being with Steve.

What dripped down was the unimportant stuff, like a traditional wedding. I don't need to show the world or Steve that I am committed to him, or he to me. Besides, if I were going to spend a lot of money and a lot of time organizing an event, I would coordinate a fund-raiser for ALS research. So I tell my friends, "Don't go planning my wedding shower just yet"—after all, I don't need two toaster ovens and a fondue set. I just need a cure.

Chapter Fourteen

FALLING
January 2004

I began falling almost a year ago. At first the falls were infrequent, once every few weeks or so. Since then, I've fallen on driveways, in parking lots, on kitchen floors, brick sidewalks, and airport walkways. Every time, I am caught unawares; it is not until one of my hip bones makes full contact with the concrete or bricks or wood floor that I realize that I've fallen again. Every time, it hurts a little more, partly because there's less flesh covering my hands and hips, partly because each fall scrapes open the recently healed scar on my left knee, partly because each time it's a little harder to get up on my own. Sometimes, though, if I'm lucky, I'm with Steve and he quickly and matter-of-factly hauls me to my feet before it even registers with me that I've fallen. Again.

I trip because I have what is known as a foot drop; the muscles in my right leg can't lift my foot the way legs normally do. To compensate, I've taken to lifting the leg higher than usual; I look a little like a lopsided majorette who lost the parade. Even so, I fall, on average, every other week, and this, not surprisingly, has made me a slow, cautious walker who constantly stares down, surveying the ground for things I could trip on. Because of this, I am now a champion beach glass collector, but the downside is that I miss a lot of the scenery unless I stop walking and look up.

Back in September, I decided that every time I fell, I would buy myself a treat: a laptop, swanky mittens, a polar fleece jacket, a pair of jeans. It was a sort of reverse psychology: I was trying to condition myself to like falling, since I do it so often. Recently, however, I discontinued this practice, as it was getting too expensive.

My most recent fall, the fall that convinced me to get a foot brace, happened at my parents' house. I was trying to get past the dog, around the fridge. Unbeknownst to me, my right foot didn't lift, and before I knew it, I was on the floor, twisted around myself. The linoleum was hard, and it hurt when first my knee, then my hip, then my upper body made contact with it. Of course, my knee wound reopened and bled all over yet another pair of jeans, and of course I was surprised, once again, to find myself prone. I couldn't help myself: I swore, loudly, and then I started crying. I didn't hold back. I let myself cry for all the falls I've had, for the hardness of floors and for the uncertainty of feet. And when my dad rushed in from the living room and gathered me in his arms and cried with me, I let him.

A few days later, I got a foot brace from my physical therapist. It's fairly lightweight, mostly Velcro, and fits under my jeans and in my sneaker. When I'm putting it on, I hold my foot pointing up and out, and pull the strap of the brace tight across my foot. Bound up this way, my foot looks like something from the pictures I've seen of Chinese foot binding. I look at it and think of the American women who have cosmetic surgery on their feet to fit into high heels, and I want to offer to trade—*Here, take my foot. You can have it. In return, I'll take yours and treat it nicely.*

So I wear the brace, hating that I've given in, hating that I've let the ALS win this round. But I feel safer. I walk faster. I don't fear falling as much. And so the other day I spoke with my physical therapist about getting a better brace, one that's more plastic than Velcro and thus offers even more support—and, I must confess, I'm looking forward to getting it.

A few months ago, I could never have imagined being excited about a foot brace. I could never have imagined myself needing a brace to walk *slowly*. I would have thought I wouldn't be able to be happy if I wasn't active. Back then, I would have described myself as always on the go. Independent. Self-reliant. Fast-moving. Indeed, I used to walk fast with my head held high. I used to walk with urgency.

These days, I walk with caution. But I'm starting to understand that the world is lovely and interesting no matter the speed you travel through it, and I know now that an orthopedic device on my leg does not make me less of a person. If anything, it's fair to say I'm stronger now—wearing a brace does that.

Lately I've been thinking about all the beach glass I've been picking up on my walks. That beach glass, I've decided, is an apt metaphor for my life. Once I was whole; then the ALS diagnosis shattered me. Now I am busy collecting the sea-worn pieces of my former self. And as I gather them up, I can't help but admire their beauty and their soft edges—and their ability to survive the pounding waves and the hard slam against rocks and that final sweep onto the beach.

Chapter Fifteen

DRIVING
January 2004

My boyfriend's driving me crazy. No, he's already driven me there, jumped out, and left me in the car, motor running, two tires flat.

Of course, he'll tell you the opposite, that it's *me* who is driving *him* crazy. He'd be partly right: it takes two people to argue. In any case, lately we've fought about our future, about blood tests, about bathroom tile, and about where the washer and dryer should go in our new home. We argue over who won the last argument, who's won the most arguments, and who's winning the one we're having.

There's no doubt we're stressed. A lot has happened since we started corresponding in early June. By mid-October and our fifth visit together, I had a diagnosis.

Since then, Steve has moved across the country, sold his house, gotten a new job, and given up his cat and proximity to his friends to be with a woman with a terminal illness. Myself, I have given up my teaching career, given Steve my power of attorney, planned my funeral, and written up my health-care directive.

Stressed? Yeah, we're stressed.

And because Steve is the closest person to me, he gets a lot of my anger. Like when people say unintentionally cruel stuff to me—I don't call them on it. Instead, I get on the phone and rant to Steve about what the person said.

In December, we talked about my taking antidepressants, thinking that the anger was a form of depression. I decided not to, though, with Steve's blessing. After all, as he pointed out, "You come by your anger fairly." It made more sense to let the anger work its way out of my body just as gradually as it worked its way into my life.

And slowly, it has. But this doesn't stop the disagreements. Because we are both worn thin from worry, what might spark a simple discussion among other couples can set off a forest fire of fighting with us.

Of all people, I should know better than to fight. I remind myself of how empty my world would be without Steve, how impossible it would be to live without him, how much I love him, and I feel ashamed. Why am I arguing with him, I who have no guarantee that I will live forever?

But why do I single myself out? Haven't we all got death sentences? As the saying goes, no one is getting out of here alive. For that matter, then, why do any of us fight with our significant others? Why do we forget to be grateful for what and whom we've got?

I think back to this past Thanksgiving, when fourteen of my friends and family sat around a large table before a large meal. Starting with the host, we each recounted what we were thankful for. Many mentioned how grateful they were to be together, or how grateful they were to be in that room, but when it was Steve's eighty-year-old father's turn, he simply said, "I'm just grateful to be anywhere." Talk about appreciating what you've got.

It's been about two months since he said that, but his words have stayed with me, and remind me of the time I spent as a temp at the Sister Kenny Institute in Minneapolis. I was twenty-three then, and assigned to a unit where brain-injured people relearned life skills. I remember well the day a young guy, not much older than I, came in and proudly reported that he'd dressed that morning all by himself.

At the time, I'd thought: *Good God, how pathetic to be excited about getting dressed.* Back then, I used to look at folks with different disabilities and feel sorry for them. I used to think the worst thing that could happen to me would be to be unable to use my legs and arms, and to be dependent on others. Back then, I thought nothing of it when I got up in the morning and dressed myself. I wasn't the slightest bit grateful.

Now, more than ten years later, I still fear losing the use of my body and being dependent on others, but I've learned how much I have in common with the young man on the brain-injury floor. I'm slowly losing the ability to do things I used to do, and I'm taking longer to do things that I used to speed through. The other day, flushed with pride from something, I don't remember what—starting Steve's car by myself? Unlocking our back door on my first try? Dressing myself in a shirt with lots of buttons?— I realized that I no longer feel sorry for folks who have physical challenges, and I certainly don't want anyone to ever feel sorry for me.

This doesn't mean that I don't freak out when I can't do something as efficiently as I used to—but I have found that when you are in danger of losing basic skills, you tend not to focus as much on what you've lost but rather on what you've got left. I know how lucky I am to be alive, to get up and dress myself, to slide that hard button through the little buttonhole without help, to pull up the zipper on my jeans with my own hand, to slide a shirt down over my head without assistance. I also know how fortunate I am to rake leaves, to move my gearshift and drive my own car, to shovel snow, to grate cheese, to slide on nylons, to use the bathroom by myself, to turn on lights. To swallow water. How, I wonder sometimes, did I ever take these things for granted?

And how, for that matter, how do I ever dare take Steve—my dear, sweet Steve, my true love—for granted?

Chapter Sixteen

TESTING
Late January 2004

Here's a memory I can see as clearly as if it had happened yesterday: it is a warm Maine day, summer 2003. I am walking down Commercial Street in Portland's Old Port, headed toward Standard Baking, where I will buy half a dozen sweet rolls to take to my father.

Coming toward me, on my side of the street, is a woman, slightly older than I, holding the hand of a young—maybe four years old?—boy. The woman walks funny; she has an uneven, halting gait and each step almost propels her up rather than forward.

They walk toward me in the early morning sunlight, and I am spellbound by how very beautiful they are.

* * *

Here's another memory, this one a bit foggier: on a cold morning in the fall of 2003, I go to church with my friend Lorraine; we've been trying out churches for awhile, trying to find one that is a good fit for both of us. This morning we're at a Methodist church not far from my house; I've been to it twice and like the minister. This morning, to my disappointment, he's on vacation.

As usual, I pray that the ALS will burn out and that I will get pregnant. Then we turn to the morning's Bible readings. It seems to me, church novice that I am, that the day's readings were chosen randomly, by someone else, before they had a substitute minister lined up, because his sermon does not relate, not in the least, to the readings.

One of the readings is from Samuel, the first book. It is the story of Hannah, of how she was barren, wanted a child, finally conceived, and then named the child Samuel. How odd that we would go to this church, today; that I would pray my usual prayer; and that this would be the morning reading. *What a coincidence*, I think.

* * *

January 2004 brings a cold spell to Portland. It is so cold that I limit my trips outdoors, and huddle instead by my sunlamp. When I brave the cold, it is only wrapped in many layers of fleece and down. I keep the heat high, and long for summer.

And I wish, hope, pray that I won't get my period. I feel like Hannah, desperate for a child. But unfortunately, I'm bloated, bloated, bloated—Stay Puft Marshmallow Man Bloated. And I'm tired, too. And I've got a little crop of acne developing. All these, I know, are signs I'm due to get my period.

So all morning I monitor my body, checking for signs the way others monitor the Dow Jones, my tampons ready. By late afternoon, it hasn't started. As an act of hope, on my way to the pool, I buy a pregnancy test.

In the women's locker room, I go into the handicapped stall and wait for the test to work its magic. Minutes pass, then the line indicating I am pregnant appears and I start beaming. I walk to the pool, but swimming is almost impossible; I'll go to breathe and inhale a handful of water. I'll try to keep track of my laps and all I'll think is, *I'm pregnant, I'm pregnant, I'm pregnant.*

What if I've made a mistake, though? What if I've done the test wrong?

On the way home, I buy another test. This time the line is really faint, but there is no getting around it. I am pregnant.

Or am I? I mean, the line is *faint.*

At my afternoon appointment, I tell my acupuncturist that I think that I am pregnant. She tells me to do a pregnancy test, just to be sure. I tell her that I already did two, but fear I did them incorrectly.

"All you have to do," she tells me, "is pee on a stick. You're pregnant."

Oh, but what if the two tests are wrong? I mean, I *want* this baby. I want children with a want that is often bigger than I am. And I most certainly do not want to get my hopes all up, only to find out that my period is simply late and that I did the tests incorrectly.

After acupuncture, I buy one last kit. This one comes with two tests, so I do them both, following the directions perfectly. Then I line them up on the tub's edge and wait.

This time, the lines are clear. I promptly call Steve and tell him the news. I am, most definitely, no doubt about it, pregnant.

* * *

I've been told by a psychic that the child is a healthy boy; I can't help it. In my head, I start calling the baby Samuel.

I've also been told that there's a 3 percent chance that I may have the gene linked to ALS, the *SOD1*; if I do, there's a 50 percent chance that the child will get ALS. Overall, that's a 1.5 percent chance that this child will have ALS. So four days after the pregnancy test escapades, I have yet another test: this time my blood is drawn and shipped to Massachusetts General, where they will study it for the *SOD1*. The tests are comprehensive and take six to eight weeks.

In the meantime, I try to focus on having a healthy baby, to send happy vibes to my body. I try to recall the excitement of the first few days when I knew I was pregnant. But sometimes, I stare at my date book in despair. There, the weeks are numbered off, each one moving me closer to the results of the blood test. Six to eight weeks seems like an awfully long time.

* * *

I've been told often since my diagnosis about the power of positive thinking, of how visualization works miracles. In imagining themselves healthy and long-lived, in imagining a future, people add time to their lives. I'm told, too, that optimism helps heal.

The optimism I have no problem with, especially now, knowing that my body, even with its death sentence, is nurturing a life.

Besides optimism, I have three images I return to. One is of an older me and an older Steve sitting on the dock at my uncle's house at Long Pond. It's a warm summer night and the moon is out. There's an old black standard poodle (one of the few breeds I'm not allergic to) between us, not the fancy poodle kind. It's just the two of us because our two high-school-age kids opted to hang out with friends, not uncool parents.

In another, Steve and I are at Willard Beach in South

Portland. We're wearing swimsuits and hats and sunscreen, and because it is a nice day, the beach is crowded. We don't seem to notice, though, because we are intent on the water, the warm sand, and our young child between us.

Here's my third image: I am walking down a street in the sunlight, four or five years from now. My gait is funny, slow, uneven, but I'm moving forward, and holding my hand is a young boy, maybe four or five. We are on our way to the bakery, for sweet rolls for him and his dad, an olive focaccia to go with our dinner, and a cup of coffee for me.

Chapter Seventeen

CLEANING

Early February 2004

Before I got ALS, I didn't know what it was. Now, after several months of research, I know more about it than I'd like to know. I know, for example, that ALS is an orphan disease. According to Hope Happens, an organization dedicated to funding research for ALS and other neurological diseases, an orphan disease is any disease that affects fewer than 200,000 people in the United States at any given time. Their Web site also claims that there are 6,000 orphan diseases that affect 25 million Americans, and that pharmaceutical companies and biotechs rarely pursue treatment of these diseases because so few people have them.[1]

In the course of my research, I've also learned that ALS

has been around for a while. Indeed, the first mention of ALS was in the 1830s, in French and British medical literature, and in 1874, a French physician, Jean-Martin Charcot, established the clinical and pathological characteristics of ALS and gave it its name. Rumor has it that he once hired a housemaid with ALS so that he could study her.[2]

I've thought often of this maid ever since I read about her. Did she know that she had ALS and that her employer was studying her? I like to think that she did, and that she didn't think too highly of Charcot for not being straight with her. In my fantasy, I see her spitting in Charcot's soup and taking cleaning shortcuts, like not sweeping under beds. She kept working for him, I decided, because she knew he was a brilliant doctor, and she hoped, desperately, that what he learned from her would benefit countless others, and maybe even cure the disease.

I think of Charcot's maid at the oddest times, such as today, as I do laundry at Steve's Colorado home. This home of his, this lovely bungalow, is on the market; in a little over a week, movers will pack up pretty much everything in this house and drive it across the country, to Maine, to our new home. But before that happens, we will have clean laundry.

This is my only household chore. It's self-imposed, too. Other than doing the laundry, there is nothing else for me to do here to be helpful. Steve's house needs very little cleaning; twice a month, his two cleaning ladies come in, and Steve returns home to a shiny teapot and spotless counters. So I leave the cleaning to them, and tackle the laundry, wondering, all the while, how it will be when we move in together in a few weeks, sans cleaning ladies.

Before Steve, I worked full-time as a teacher. When I dated, it was usually in or near my own income bracket, and I always figured that if I was ever in a long-term relationship, we'd find a way to divvy up the household tasks. Sometimes I fantasized about being a stay-at-home mom, raising a bunch of kids while canning, cooking, and cleaning, but as I approached thirty-four, I became increasingly convinced that I was destined to be a single, working parent.

But I'm with Steve now, and he and I weren't in the same income bracket before I stopped working; he is a doctor and I was a teacher. Now the wage gap between us is wider than the Atlantic. And I'm staying home, all right, but I struggle to figure out how I can contribute, how I will find equal footing in a relationship I am entering at a financial disadvantage. Mind you, this is my issue—it doesn't seem to keep Steve up at night—but if I want my contribution to our relationship, in lieu of money, to be household management, and in particular, cleaning, how will I ever do it? I'm not as agile as I used to be, and as it is, cleaning my three-room, first-floor apartment takes planning and time. How will I clean a whole house by myself?

Perhaps this is why I am so fixated on the rumor about Charcot: I want to have my own ALS cleaning lady. I'd like one my age because it would be so nice to have someone female and young to talk with about this ALS stuff, someone who would know where I'm coming from. That's one of the problems, I'm finding, with having an orphan disease: there aren't a lot of you.

So I recently posted a query on an ALS chat site, seeking other young women with ALS. One woman, also in her thirties, responded. She lives in Florida, has children, and used to be physically active. I've received two e-mails from her, and both times, it was like finding a twin I'd been separated from since birth. It's hard being around able-bodied people all the time, people who don't have terminal illnesses. Some days, I feel an aloneness that's bigger, meaner, more all-encompassing than anything I've ever known. I don't ever remember feeling this way before September 15. These days, I find many situations stressful, unless close friends or family are around. I never know when I'll hear an unintentionally hurtful remark. I never know when someone will feel sorry for me, something that irritates me more than an eyelash in a contact lens. I understand that the people who make these comments and behave this way just don't know how to respond to my life changes, but still, their comments or insinuations sting.

My fantasy ALS maid, by contrast, would understand.

And you know, I'll bet we could be pretty efficient, even though I imagine we'd talk a lot as we scrubbed floors and vacuumed rugs and cleaned bathrooms. Perhaps we could clean my house one week and hers the next, just the two of us, working together—just like Steve's Colorado cleaning ladies, only different.

There's another reason, I fear, that I'm so fixated on Charcot's supposed maid. There's a nagging worry in my brain that I was she in another life. Maybe that explains why I love dishwashers and the smell of Pine-Sol and Murphy Oil Soap. Maybe that explains why I don't mind doing laundry. And maybe, just maybe, that explains my endless frustration that there is still no cure for this disease— not even after all that cleaning.

Chapter Eighteen

EXPECTING

February 2004

One morning in late January, Steve and I woke up early. We'd just returned to Denver from a week-long vacation and were still on St. Croix time: when my cell phone rang at 7:19 AM, Steve was already at work in his office, and I was fighting morning sickness with crackers and ginger tea. Quickly I did the time zone math: 9:19 AM on the east coast—business hours. Who could it be?

It was the genetic counselor we'd consulted before getting pregnant and in the early weeks of the pregnancy.

"The test results came in last week," the genetic counselor said. "You don't have the *SOD1* mutation. From now on, you're a normal pregnancy," she continued. "And you're not thirty-five or older, so there's no need for the amniocentesis."

I was turning off my cell phone as I approached Steve's office. "Steve," I said from the doorway, "I don't have it, the *SOD1* mutation. The baby's going to be OK."

And then I started crying.

* * *

Since getting the test results and since confirming that I'm pregnant, I've experienced a range of different emotions. There's the joy that we're pregnant and there's the relief that I don't have the *SOD1* gene mutation. There's the surprise, too: we never expected that I would get pregnant so quickly, so easily. As a result, I think often of this child as a gift, given to us in the days before Christmas.

Besides the joy and surprise and relief, there's also the ongoing mystery: between the ALS and the pregnancy, my body is constantly changing. I never know what to expect—and there's really nowhere to turn to find out, because there isn't a lot of literature for the expecting ALS mom. The books about ALS never mention pregnancy, and the two articles about ALS and pregnancy were written for doctors and are downright dire.

When I turned to pregnancy books, I found nothing better. Of the ones I own, only one mentions disability and pregnancy; it's given a few paragraphs. It's probably just as well; I have a hard time reading most pregnancy books because I get annoyed at the assumption that we are all happily married heterosexual women. What I'm finding is that until *What to Expect When You're Expecting for the ALS Mom Regardless of Whether She Is Married or Not* comes out in print, I'm better off avoiding both the ALS books and the pregnancy books and saving my questions instead for my capable doctors and nurses.

In the meantime, I forge my way through the ALS pregnancy.

* * *

When friends talk about their pregnancies, they speak fondly of their midwives. When Steve and I tried to get pregnant, I didn't think about the fact that, as a nurse told me, "No midwife would *ever* want to take you on."

But I made peace with that, thanks, in large part, to the excellent medical practice that did agree to take me on. But then, a few weeks into the pregnancy, I was told that my doctor, whom I adore, trust, and respect, might not be able to be with me at the hospital when I gave birth. Instead I might have a doctor (most likely male) from the on-call group. Since then, I've gotten to know, like, and trust a male doctor at the practice, but I haven't had a chance to meet the other male doctors in the practice or in the on-call group. I am sure these are all good doctors.

I know some excellent male doctors (Steve among them), and I completely understand that my doctor needs time off—but still, I freaked out.

I've had my share of bad experiences with men. Mind you, these involved a small minority of the male population, and I know there are some incompetent women doctors, too. But when I'm naked and vulnerable, I can't help it: I want a woman doctor. I remember the old man who forced his tongue in my mouth when I was twenty, the middle-aged friend of our family who felt me up when I was nineteen, the young guy who nearly forced me into sex when I was in eighth grade—and although I know full well that not all men are like this, I also know that a woman has never done any of those things to me.

So when I was told the news about the doctor situation, I started thinking: What if, heaven forbid, I can't talk by the time I deliver? One of the weird, wicked, and wonderful things about ALS is that you lose functions faster than the average person, yet not so fast that you don't gradually get used to the change and prepare for it. I've ignored the changes to my voice for months, chalking them up to stress, allergies, the planets being out of line, and talking too much, but there's no more denying that it's hard to listen to myself: I don't sound like me anymore. First, there's the abundance of saliva in my mouth; it's like trying to talk underwater. Then there's the fact that my voice is slower, more slurred. I have to be mindful of speaking clearly so that I am understood. If I'm nervous or upset, my voice goes high, as if it's projecting out of the top of my mouth, like a cartoon character. And if I talk too much, I lose my voice, which puts me in an odd position: I hate the sound of my voice, but I desperately fear the loss of it.

But even more, I fear getting a doctor I don't know the day I deliver, and being unable to speak. I have a hard enough time getting my needs met and being respected *with* a voice. If I'm naked, vulnerable, and unable to speak, I want a doctor I *know*.

It's hard to explain this to people, and even if I knew some women who had ALS and had given birth, it'd be hard to make comparisons, since ALS affects everyone differently. I try to talk pregnancy with other non-ALS women, but am almost always aware that I am not "normal," that they aren't considering getting handicapped plates or worrying about using a wheelchair at the end of their pregnancies.

However, the more I talk to other women, the more obvious it becomes that there are few "normal" pregnancies. Among the four pregnant women I know, we've all had our share of scares and fears. I don't take pleasure in their trials, but I do take solace in the fact that even in its unusualness, my pregnancy is still "normal."

* * *

But sometimes I can't help it: I lust after others' lives. Like the morning Steve and I were eating breakfast on a patio not far from a St. Croix beach. In front of us, at the water's edge, was a young couple with a little boy and a little girl. I watched them play in the sand and try out a sailboat as I waited for my pancakes, and I could not help it. I got envious. I wanted *that* for *us*.

Once, when Steve and I began talking about starting a family, someone asked me if I was prepared to be a different kind of mother than I'd always imagined. It was a good question—I always figured I'd be the mom who plays basketball with her kids and bikes and hikes and swims with them. The kind of mom who never sits still.

I probably won't ever be that kind of mother, but I know now that there are all kinds of mothers. I remind myself that the qualities that will make me a good mother are qualities I haven't lost with the ALS; that if anything, they've only gotten stronger. Instead of running off to play Frisbee with the kids, I will be able to sit and listen as they discuss their day. *Let Steve run with them* is my new philosophy.

But even so, when I look at "normal" families, like the family on the beach, I am envious. Then I get firm with myself: if I were to trade lives with them, I'd have to take everything about their lives, not just the good or the surface appearance.

Besides, and more important, I tell myself, there is no use wasting time mourning what I haven't lost.

* * *

My clothes stopped fitting a few months into the pregnancy, so I convinced Steve to go to the mall with me.

"I never imagined I'd ever go into one of these stores," Steve says as we walk into the maternity store, and I agree. I've never imagined myself pregnant, although I've often pictured myself with kids.

This day, I'm looking for two pairs of pants, and Steve waits while I, according to him, "try on everything in the store."

I hate the mall, as a general rule, but this day, I don't mind it. I don't mind my legs, either, even though they're wobbly from too much standing. I ignore the world outside the mall, the rain we will have to dash through to get to the car, and the many fears I can obsess over at a moment's notice. Instead, I focus on us, the three of us. I am surprised to be looking at elastic-waisted jeans, drunk on happiness and elation, and stunned by my good fortune.

Chapter Nineteen

MOVING
February 2004

If you knew me, you would know about The Great Purple Couch Escapade. It's one of those stories that is firmly embedded in the family/friend folklore, and hauled out at moments when the conversation lags. "Remember the purple couch?" someone will ask, and then launch into the story: how once, after my significant other of four years moved out, leaving me with an empty house, I broke down and bought a couch. It was the first piece of furniture I'd ever bought new, and I agonized for months about buying it. I sat on couches all over greater Portland, grilled furniture associates, sat on more couches, and finally bought a blackberry-colored velvet-like couch with lots of pillows. The couch was nicer than my car, and I loved it in a way other people love their kids or their pets.

When I moved three months after purchasing my couch, it was to a third-floor, loftlike attic apartment. I signed the lease and thought about how happy my big purple couch and I would be snuggled under the skylights and eaves.

But on moving day, my fantasy was shattered. I'd recruited friends and family to help, but try as we might, we couldn't get the couch into the apartment. We tried the back door, the front door, and hoisting it up to the little roof just above the sunporch. We took off the legs, we took off the cushions. And we pushed.

Nothing worked. A few weeks later, I sold the couch.

Four years have passed since then, and I've recently moved again, only this time into a house with Steve. Friends and relatives once again lugged boxes and furniture, and sure as you can count on snow in Maine in February, someone had to mention The Great Purple Couch Escapade, a story Steve can practically recite along with them—and we've known each other only nine months.

Now that all our belongings are in the new house, we've begun furniture/decorating negotiations. A friend recently told me about a couple she knew who went to counseling before they moved in together because their styles were so different. The counselor recommended a consultation with an interior designer. Steve and I did neither.

As a result, we spent more time debating the colors of

our tiles and walls than I spent studying for some of my college exams. Furniture negotiations were just as intense.

My secondhand gold, green, and rust paisley-patterned love seat and my secondhand green paisley curved-back chair don't match Steve's bachelor plaid couch or swanky overstuffed green sofa or grown-up-style coffee table, so after much negotiation, we moved the sofa to my study and the chair to the upstairs hall. But with them gone, most of the furniture on the first floor is Steve's. I love his furniture—even his plaid couch is growing on me—but his style isn't my style. He's got classic taste; he likes wood and Mission-style furniture. By contrast, my furniture is a mixture of stuff from my grandmother's and from the secondhand store; I favor colors and patterns. Steve's idea of matching is pretty traditional; woods, greens, navys. My idea of matching is when all the furniture in a room came from the same consignment shop.

Sitting on Steve's couch, I realized that I wanted a couch that I'd been with since its beginning, just as Steve had been with his. I wanted something big and comfortable, something that was my style of furniture, in a color that I like. So I went to the purple couch store.

It had been four years, and I knew the couch wouldn't be there. So I tried all the couches in the store, taking note of two that were OK, but nothing like the purple couch. I was getting ready to leave when I decided to do one last sweep, and there, in the back of the store, against a green backdrop, was the purple couch. I couldn't believe it. It was like unexpectedly running into an ex you shouldn't have broken up with. It was like being offered chocolate cake after a four-year diet of tofu. It was like destiny.

Steve, naturally, wasn't as excited as I was about my find. But I glowed all afternoon. It's only a couch, I know, but on my lifeline, it represented Incomplete Business, and getting it back—or buying its twin—felt like the first step in closing that gap.

Steve puts up with a lot, living with me, but surely he, given his line of work, understands the need for closure. So, I think to myself, maybe he won't mind if once that couch gets here, I get off it only to shower, eat, and fluff the pillows.

Chapter Twenty

DUMPING
March 2004

For as long as I can remember, Saturday has been Dad's Dump Day. Sometime after breakfast, he fills up his car and drives a couple of miles down Route 4 to the dump, where he sorts his recyclables into bins and disposes of his trash. He's pretty careful, because the attendants at his dump take recycling seriously, and they know if you're recycling because all the garbage has to be in clear bags, so you can't pull a fast one.

Around the holidays last year, the dump attendants issued their version of a holiday card, a white, photocopied sheet wishing people a good holiday and reminding them to separate all their bows, ribbons, Styrofoam, plastic, and foil wrappings and to break down all their corrugated cardboard. I'll admit, when I saw the "Holiday Reminder" hanging on my parents' fridge, I was envious. I was a city-living renter then, and I wanted a dump where I could sort corrugated cardboard. I wanted to feel righteous and environmentally friendly, too.

My wish was granted. A few weeks ago, after we moved in and started unpacking our belongings, we watched Mount St. Cardboard grow and waited for garbage day. Finally, when our trash pile reached larger-than-life proportions, Steve took action.

"What day is garbage day?" he asked a neighbor who'd stopped by to welcome us to the neighborhood.

"Garbage day," said the neighbor with a pause, "is any day you want it to be."

We needed, he told us, to take our garbage to the local dump.

So a few days later, Steve loaded up his car with bags and boxes while I scanned the phone book, trying to find a listing for the dump. I finally stumbled on the phrase "transfer station." That sounded familiar, so I asked the man who answered the phone, "Are you the place formerly known as the dump?"

They were, and after I got directions, Steve was on his way. He chose to take what is now known in our household as The Scenic Dump Route, following the shoreline, and in the days that followed, he made four more runs. Not to be outdone, I volunteered to go, loaded up my car, and took a more utilitarian route through suburbs and countryside. It was early afternoon, midweek, and the place was hopping. After I'd recycled my cardboard and thrown my trash down the chute, I lugged my boxes of books and castaways over to the dump's Swap Shop. There, a woman quickly scanned the titles, gathered up my books, and put them in her car. My blender was taken by another woman and a man grabbed my plastic frog. I returned home with a garbage-free car and a large, second-hand plant pot—something I'd been meaning to pick up at Home Depot.

Since then, I've been trying to figure out what I've come to call my Transfer Station Fixation. I think it boils down to three things. First, and most obvious, it's easy for me to appreciate the dump because Steve is our main dump liaison, i.e., does all the work, by virtue of his stronger arms and larger car.

The second reason is because I get giddy when I see the neat bins lined up and ready for cardboard, tin cans, plastics, papers. At the dump, there is a place for everything. This is reassuring to me: living in a society that throws a lot away—including perfectly good people, like the elderly and disabled—is a challenge for me since my diagnosis, and it's reassuring to spend time at the local dump, where, as the Swap Shop's success shows, almost everything has value. Indeed, at a dump like my parents', very little is thrown away.

I've thought about this a lot lately, thanks to being pregnant and having ALS. I've been surprised by all the testing that is done to the fetus and mother. I'm more pro-choice than Gloria Steinem, but when I hear people talk about having the amniocentesis at week twenty and considering terminating certain pregnancies, I get sort of sad, and then relieved: I am so glad that my parents couldn't test to see if I had ALS, that they didn't consider terminating me.

I also feel a twinge of sympathy for what these expecting parents are going through, and I understand that we all have different approaches to this issue. It's one that Steve and I struggled with, too. The weeks I waited for the *SOD1* test results were as agonizing as the four weeks I waited for my ALS diagnosis, and I was conflicted about what to do. My opinion changed during this time; before ALS I would have, no doubt about it, terminated an ALS pregnancy. However, the longer I had my diagnosis, the more I began to value my own life. Even though it now is an ALS life, I don't see it as any less valuable than an Average-Person-Without-ALS's life. However, I still struggled with the ethics of it all; if I passed on the ALS to my offspring, we feared the child would get it at a younger age than I did. Fortunately—that word is such an understatement—Steve and I didn't have to deal with these questions.

Perhaps, however, the main reason I like the dump is

because everyone in town has to go there. Sure, a handful of people may pay private companies to deal with their garbage, but almost everyone else fills their car up Saturday morning and queues up for the trash chute. The dump, as I see it, is the small-town equalizer.

My point was proven well at my parents' dump a little while ago. A fairly important and influential man went to the dump near closing one night and somehow managed to throw out two bags of garbage—two *black bags* of garbage, that is—without getting caught. But later that night, after he'd returned home, he got a call from one of the attendants. They'd found his bags and opened them, figured out whose trash it was, and wanted to let him know that he'd used up his one "home free" pass, and it'd be no more Mr. Nice Guy on their end if he tried such tomfoolery again.

Chapter Twenty-one

BRACING
March 2004

Not to brag or anything, but I am the Queen of Braces. I have tried several types of foot braces: First, I had a soft, mostly Velcro brace. Then I tried a whole bunch of other braces, and finally settled on a generic, over-the-counter, anti-foot-drop device; it looked like an elongated shoehorn. It was plastic and extended up the back of my leg, and attached with material that looked like an athletic bandage. In addition to being uncomfortable, it also chafed at my much-too-small calf, conducted cold, and cut into my foot when I walked.

ALS has been around for a long time, but you'd never guess it to look at this device or at the handful of other over-the-counter braces available. The husband of a friend of mine who has ALS once warned me that all the devices I would be given would be poorly made, the assumption being that people only use them for a little while, then get better. Those of us who are getting worse simply make do. I didn't believe him then, but now I do. All it took was five minutes wearing the elongated shoehorn and I knew that no one would wear it for long.

Including me. I gave the brace a try, then returned to see my physical therapist. "How is the foot brace working out?" she asked, and told me that she was trying to sell another patient of hers on getting one.

"It sucks," I said, and told her how it chafed and cut and conducted.

"Well, what do you think of this new brace?" the orthopedic specialist asked, trying another over-the-counter model on my foot. I looked down at the little piece of plastic on the outside of my sneaker, tucked under my laces. It dug into my leg and did not appear to be lifting my foot up.

"It sucks," I said again, and both my therapist and the orthotics specialist laughed. One of them told me that I might not want to consider a career as a motivational speaker.

But my complaining worked. I recently graduated to the king of foot braces—a custom-made Ankle Foot Orthotic (AFO). The AFO is a serious brace; at the orthotic place they made casts of my feet, and then, three weeks later, I had foot-to-calf braces for each leg. I could have ordered a camouflage pattern on my braces, or mama and papa bears, or martians, but I went with a blue fish design because it reminded me of summer, and of swimming.

My brace-wearing isn't restricted to my feet; I also have a hand brace. I got it because my right hand is getting weaker, beginning to atrophy; it resembles the hand of a ninety-year-old. Already the loose skin is starting to pile up at my knuckles so that my fingers look like a little elephant's legs. (It's mighty attractive, let me tell you.)

Because of this muscle loss, my hand's inclination is to curl; already one finger is permanently bent. At night, I wake up and find my hand bunched into a fist, my nails digging into my palm. For a few weeks, I tried wearing a bike glove to bed; the padded palm saved me from dig marks, but still, the hand curled. Then, the other night, I woke up and found my left hand in a tight fist. Sympathy curl, I told Steve. Brace time, I told myself.

So my occupational therapist made me a brace from some hard white plastic material. It starts below my wrist and extends up to my fingers; there's a thumb holder, too. The top of the brace is open, and wide straps affix to Velcro and hold it on my hand. I've never seen anything like it, and it's actually not that uncomfortable, as braces go.

And yet—I haven't worn it. I've had it for sixteen hours, and still, it sits on my desk. It makes me nervous:

on my hand, it's a weapon. I fear half-waking up some night, discovering that Steve's stolen the covers, and, before I realize what I've done, whacking him with my super-brace. It's really a small wonder he wants to sleep with me at all, with or without the weapon. Between my three pregnancy pee runs per night and my infrequent teeth grinding, I am not a very attractive bedfellow. And now I come armed.

My neuromuscular specialist says this hand business is just one of the many fun side effects of ALS, and it was at my five-month checkup that he recommended the hand brace. He also said that there was no significant change since he'd last seen me—except in my left foot, fingers, and right hand.

His assessment didn't surprise me. Even before the appointment, I knew the fingers were getting worse. Every day, it seems, I discover a new skill that fingers are useful for, a skill I no longer have: opening a Ziploc bag, turning on a lamp, undoing a twisty tie, writing with a pen, putting on lip liner or earrings with backs, doing basic nail care, stapling, giving back rubs, unlocking a door, buttoning a shirt.

I'm learning, though, that with a little ingenuity, I can still do many of these tasks. I tear open bags with my teeth and one hand. I use clothespins (held between my teeth) instead of twisty ties. I turn on an overhead light with a switch instead of using a lamp. I use two hands, my upper body, and a few cuss words to turn the key in the ignition or rotate the washing machine dial. I stopped wearing lip liner and giving back rubs. Steve puts in my earrings and opens containers for me. I lock my mouth around the childproof Listerine, squeeze with my teeth, and turn it with my hands, hoping I don't get my lips caught. I go to acupuncture, and that buys me some relief, as well.

Doing my nails, however, has been the biggest challenge. I borrowed some special nail clippers from my friend, but they're more suited to trimming a giant's nose hairs, so I soon gave up—and gave in to manicures.

In the past, you would never have considered me the type of girl who gets her nails done, but even in my hike-a-mountain-by-myself days, I loved getting a manicure. Back then, it was a rare indulgence. These days, it's a practicality, so I don't fight it anymore, nor do I feel guilty about the cost; after all, I go to a cheap chain or a beauty school. If I didn't have the ugly side effects of ALS, I've decided, this disease would be a gift: I have an excuse to get my nails done.

That sounds almost flippant, I know. The real truth of my ALS is that it takes daily acts of courage to get up, live the day fully, be grateful for what I have, and to find the humor and grace and the pleasure, yes, pleasure, in not being able to clip my own nails.

* * *

After my five-month checkup, on our way to the parking

garage, I was close to crying. Sure, I told Steve, I was grateful, so grateful, for the good news—*no significant change—but what about my right hand? I kept remembering the doctor's advice to buy a program that would allow me to speak my documents into the computer, just in case I need it.* Just in case I need it? In case I can't write with my hand? How would I ever write without my hand? After I scribble notes in my journal, I type up my essays or stories and print them out, and then I revise them, by hand, and sometimes I cut them up with scissors, then type them up again. I can't imagine writing without my right hand.

But the cold, hard truth is attached to my body, and not a second passes in which I don't recognize that the right hand is getting worse. Sometimes, when I feel like having a really good panic attack, I think of my right foot, that damned useless right foot, and worry that the right hand is going the same way.

For now, I ignore the computer voice-writing program, even though it sits on the floor of my study, inches away from me. Instead, I sit down at the computer and look long and hard at my right hand. *Come on, old girl,* I say to it, and coax the fingers over the keyboard, over the letters that I love so, and then I thank them for each and every word they type.

* * *

I have fewer and fewer panic attacks the further I get from October 14, 2003. However, I still struggle with how to

live in a body that is aging so fast, a body that needs so
many braces (three at this point). When I started dating
Steve, I loved the fact that he ran, hiked, and biked; I
imagined us growing old actively together, and it's frustrating when I can't join him on a run or a long walk.
Even more annoying is that even though my body can't do
some of these things, my mind remembers how to do
them, and longs to do them again. I miss the old me the
way one mourns a predeceased partner, daily and wistfully.

It's also frustrating to be surrounded by friends my age
with whom I used to be able to keep up, but who can whip
my ass in seconds now. Many of my friendships involved
being active: we'd walk together, run together, hike
together. Some days, I feel worlds away from the life I cre-
ated before September 15, 2003, and it is on these days
that I feel the most affinity with the disabled and the elderly, who know what it feels like when your body betrays
you so suddenly, what it feels like when your own death
isn't an abstract concept.

Because of this, I can often push aside my fear and
anger and frustration about my own situation and replace
it with deep respect for those whose bodies have betrayed
them, those who face the challenges of age and disability
daily. At times like this, I look back at the able-bodied,
healthy young woman I was before September 15—she
thought she knew so much!—and I can't help but feel
sorry for her.

Chapter Twenty-two

QUESTIONING
March 2004

I t's a warmish March day, and I sit in my therapist's office, high above Portland's Exchange Street. Out her window is the bay, and from her white leather couch I watch boats coming into the harbor.

We are talking about the recent past—May 2003 until March 2004, to be exact—and I am musing about a topic new for us: religion.

I grew up Baptist—Northern Baptist. My parents and grandmother attend the North Livermore Baptist Church, and they are what I think of as Maine Religious: they have strong values and beliefs, which they are careful to keep to themselves. Although I had to attend Sunday school until I was in high school, I never felt that their religious views were forced on me.

After high school, I stayed far away from organized religion—I was frustrated by the ways people used religion to justify discrimination and meanness—but every now and then, I'd find myself attending a church, always a Methodist or Unitarian or some liberal church. I'd go for several weeks, then get too busy and stop. All along, regardless of whether or not I went, I practiced my own brand of religion, the kind that says a quick thanks to Someone for an especially nice day or a really good glass of wine.

So when I began to understand that what was wrong with me might be something bad, it was only natural that I turn to something I was familiar with, something that gave my family members strength. My grandmother calls her prayers "conversations," and that's how I've come to think of mine. In September I started conversing daily, begging for good medical news, for the leg and foot problem to go away. In October, right up to the minute of the appointment with the neuromuscular specialist, I was still conversing and trying to plea-bargain, but the "if this isn't serious, I'll become a nun" ploy didn't work.

Despite this, I've continued the conversations. When you get bad news, I think it tends to make you either an atheist (how could this happen if there is a God?) or a believer (you need some greater power to believe in). For me, it's been the latter. It gives me comfort and offers me a framework to cope with the ALS: religion has made it easier for me to think about death. I like assuming that there is a hereafter, and that in it, I will be able to run forever without cramps, I will be able to sit by a pool in the sunshine sipping a gin and tonic with my Nana as long as I want and not worry about skin cancer, and I will finally get to tell my buddy Paul, who died of AIDS early in the epidemic, that I'm sorry for not having been a better friend in his final days.

This doesn't mean, though, that I go to church regularly, that I quote Bible verses to my friends, or even that I've stopped saying "goddamn it" when I'm mad. It does mean that I've become a lot more accepting of others' religious and nonreligious views—just as long as they don't force them on me—because I know how important my own brand of Maine Religion is to me.

Since my diagnosis, a comment I've heard several times is, "What kind of God would do this to you?" It's a question I myself have asked. A lot. After all, I've been fairly good, I think, in this life: Why a terminal illness? Why not a hangnail or a sore throat?

But here's the conundrum: since June, one good thing after another has happened to me. I look at how perfect my life is now, how I've got everything I wanted, and I think, of course there's a God. Look at all these miracles.

I remember an appointment I had with my therapist months ago, when I told her, "I've been praying for a miracle, and nothing has happened."

Her response was immediate: "Darcy," she said, "your life is *charged* with miracles."

Thinking about that now and sitting in her office, I say, "So here's the dilemma. How do I account for the horror of this past year and still acknowledge the bushels of blessings and miracles that I'm getting? How do I figure out if there is a God, and who this God is?"

She is quiet, so I keep talking, and tell her about the quote by Rainer Maria Rilke a friend had sent me: "Be patient toward all that is unsolved in your heart and try to love the *questions themselves.* Do not now seek the answers, which cannot be given you because you would not be able to live them. And the point is, to live everything. *Live the questions now.*"

I tell Sara that I am learning to ask the questions.

"And there," Sara responds, "in the questions, you'll find God."

Chapter Twenty-three

RETURNING

March 2004

We were standing on the stairs, talking about the shirts Steve had received from an online company. One of them was nothing like what he'd thought it would be, and he wanted to return it, but the company charged a six-dollar return fee, unless he had one of their credit cards, in which case the shipping was free. Steve concluded that that was the problem with shopping online; things aren't always what they look like. He paused, then leaned down to touch my leg. "Except for you," he said.

We both laughed. "I don't know," I replied. "I think there are some days when you'd like to return me."

"Only if I had a matchmaker's credit card," Steve assured me, "so the shipping was free."

We were joking, but, I'll admit, there are times when I think Steve would be better off returning me, trading me in for someone healthy. I think of all he's lost in this relationship, and I wish he'd known me before the ALS, back when I was active and healthy and energetic.

And I worry about how dependent I am on him, and get frustrated with how my illness threatens the balance of our relationship. We've been together for ten months now; half of the time he's had to take care of me in some way. In the beginning, this involved translating medical information and attending appointments. Then he began lifting me up from falls. Now he helps me dress and walk and cook. Not a day passes that we don't think or talk about ALS.

When Steve first decided to move to Maine to be with me, a few people told me how lucky I was to have him, and they seemed to consider him a martyr. Since the hero needs a victim, I knew who got that part, and their comments irritated me. And while I agree that Steve is amazing, unbelievable, and doing things that I'm not sure I could do, I fear that in making him a superhero, these people made me someone to pity, someone to be rescued. Someone who should feel lucky that anybody wants to be with her. While I don't fault these people for their comments (we, too, were having a hard time adjusting to the change in our young relationship), I now know: even though I come with ALS, I am giving back just as much to Steve as he is giving to me. My having ALS doesn't make me any less attractive partner material.

This was confirmed for me at a recent ALS meeting I attended. As we introduced ourselves, the husband of a woman with ALS said, "It is such an honor to be able to take care of my wife." He was so sincere and straightforward about it that I almost cried (then I thought of a hot fudge sundae and that distracted me). *What a great husband*, I thought. Then I looked at his brave, talented wife, and thought some more. *And what a great wife he must have*, I added.

This discovery is mine alone, of course. Steve already knows all this. *I'm* the one who's just catching on.

* * *

These days, we've settled into a routine, and neither of us is sending the other one back. Our house is even starting to look like a home: pictures are on walls, piles of paperwork fill corners, our cellar is a disaster, and we've unpacked all but seven boxes.

As we've put stuff away, I've thought often of the little one—the Jelly Bean, as we've taken to calling our offspring, thanks to a friend's comment after seeing the first ultrasound—and our future family.

When I began telling people I was pregnant, I feared the reaction I would get. To my delight, almost everyone was excited; from a handful of people, though, I did get the feeling that they were taken aback. In fact, they looked shocked. A social services worker even asked if the pregnancy was planned. Maybe I read too much into their faces, comments, and body language, but I imagined they were saying to themselves, *Doesn't she know she has a terminal illness? Is she in denial? Or just selfish?*

But isn't any act of procreation selfish? I mentally replied. And aren't we all going to die someday?

Besides, we've discussed all this already. When Steve and I were considering having a baby, we talked often about my predicted disability and death. We worried about Steve tending me and our child and about him maybe ending up a single parent. What put our minds at rest was the knowledge that if anything happens, our huge support network will kick in, and Steve will have the assistance of family and friends. I'm sure they would do a fabulous job raising our child, if given the opportunity.

So I try not to worry about who will teach our child to floss and write thank-you notes and bake chocolate-chip cookies. Instead, I take the handful of weird reactions, examine them, put them in the black box I'm reserving for such things, and push it to the back of my brain. If that part of my brain is anything like our cellar, I'll forget about the box before too long.

Then I focus on the now. I refuse to stay up late worrying about dying and leaving Steve a single parent—because as far as I'm concerned, Steve, and the Jelly Bean, are stuck with me for the long haul.

No returns.

Chapter Twenty-four

HELPING
Early April 2004

S he asked for help. I was looking for veggie burgers, and she was looking for beer. She was much shorter than I, maybe 4'11"; I guessed her to be in her late sixties, maybe early seventies. She wanted to know if I'd get the six-pack of Bud Light for her, high on the top shelf, far out of her reach. After she thanked me and tucked the beer in her cart, I got my groceries and left, but I haven't stopped thinking about her since— probably because I can't help but admire how graciously she asked for help, and how graciously she thanked me for it.

I hate asking for help. I've been self-sufficient, for the most part, since graduating from college, and I've lived alone for at least seven of my thirty-four years. I am also a Mainer by birth and disposition, which is to say that I am an independent, stubborn, do-it-my-way-and-by-myself kind of woman, the sort of person who hates being dependent on others, the sort of person whose middle name is "My Way or the Highway." I'd sooner drive two hours out of my way than ask for directions, than ask for *help*.

But even though I hate accepting assistance, I am more than happy to help others. Recently a friend's mother came to town, and her plane arrived late, long after my friend's young daughter was asleep, so I offered to pick her mother up. No, my friend told me, her mom could take a cab. When her mother heard this, she immediately accepted my offer, telling her daughter to let people help when they offer. I enjoyed the half hour I spent with my friend's mother, and I felt good, knowing I'd saved her the hassle of finding a cab.

Remembering that feeling, I cannot help but ask: why is it that so many of us dislike asking for—or accepting offers of—help?

Since my diagnosis, I have been flooded with offers of assistance. I think that the hardest thing about accepting help is acknowledging that something is wrong with me. In accepting help, I admit that something is different, that something doesn't work, that I am weak, that I have ALS. I also hate to be a burden. But there is no denying that my friends want to do something, and thanks to the airport-ride and beer episodes, I understand that I need to find ways to let people help me because it will make *them* feel better. And it will be good practice for me, too—learning to accept help graciously.

A few mornings ago, I had a good chance to start practicing when Steve and I awoke to four inches of water in our outer basement. The previous owners had warned us to start the sump pump the minute spring came, but we hadn't, and that morning, when we finally got the sump hooked up, we discovered it was broken.

So I called the previous owner and asked what she would do, and within minutes she was in our basement, armed with her Shop-Vac, sump pump, shovel, and broom. As she lugged and pushed and lifted, I tried to do my part, but it was hard to watch her be so capable and strong when I couldn't be. By noon, thanks to her hard work, the basement was dry.

After she left, I went shopping to buy us some pumping paraphernalia: a hose, an industrial broom, two orange extension cords, two automatic sump pumps, and a pump that isn't automatic but pumps something like four billion gallons per minute. At both hardware stores, I had to ask the clerks to hook up the pumps for me, because I knew that when I got home there'd be no one there to help. Like the former owner of my house, the clerks willingly obliged.

These successes encouraged me, and now not a day passes that I don't ask for help. One day I asked my sister to accompany me to a reading of my work, and to fill in for me when my voice tired. Another day, before guests came over, Steve helped me dress, sliding the tiny buttons of my cardigan through the tiny holes, then putting my earrings in for me (no small feat for a guy who's never worn one) and buckling my shoes. And weeks ago, at the airport, I asked strangers to snap my backpack for me when I was traveling alone.

I've even accepted help from my sixty-year-old mom and eighty-seven-year-old grandmother. They visited one day and kept offering to do chores or tasks for me. Finally I let them arrange my office. I have little upper-body strength, but my mom and grandmother don't have a shortage. They moved my love seat, my desk, my bookshelf, and my file cabinet. Then they moved them around again. I stood by, supervising, offering encouragement, trying not to be underfoot. It was frustrating, being the weakest woman in the room, watching them work.

When they were done, the three of us sat down and admired their handiwork. "Nice job," I said, and thanked them. "No big deal," my mom told me. My gram flexed her muscles in response. "See how strong I am?" she asked, then added, "Feel my muscles."

So I did, and then complimented her—graciously, just as I imagine the woman in the grocery store would have done.

Chapter Twenty-five

MEETING
April 2004

I didn't want to go.

I avoided the ALS support group meetings in November and December (I had just gotten the diagnosis and was overwhelmed), January (I was in Colorado), and February (we were in the midst of moving). I was nervous about attending such a group, and about identifying with a subculture I hadn't chosen to join. Besides, what if I acted inappropriately? I thought back to the first person with ALS that I'd met after my diagnosis; when I saw her in her wheelchair, my eyes had teared up. She'd handled it well, but I was mortified. What if I did that at the meeting?

By March, however, I'd run out of excuses and was starting to appear pretty lame. So I went.

* * *

The group was held in a town about an hour away, and on the drive there, I made myself think of other things, anything other than the meeting I was going to attend. I didn't ask anyone to come with me because I wanted to make a quick exit if necessary, and I bribed myself into going with the promise of a vanilla shake afterward.

After the meeting came to order, we went around the room, introduced ourselves, and spoke of what we'd been doing over the past few weeks. People talked about grown children, grandchildren, retirement. I spoke of moving in with Steve, of living with our contractor, of unfinished bathrooms and unpacked boxes.

I thought about the meeting the whole way home. It had been helpful, and the people were interesting and kind, but I wasn't sure I'd return. I was, by far, the youngest person with ALS in the room, and I didn't think that I had much in common with the other people, other than the disease. I also didn't like seeing all the stages and faces of ALS. It unnerved me.

But when April came, something drew me back to the meeting. This time, when I walked into the room, several people waved or smiled at me, and when I looked around and saw the cramped hands, the leg braces, the wheel-chair, the two talking computers, the walker, and the bodies that used the devices, I understood how ALS affects everyone differently. This both upset me—how will they ever find a cure if the disease varies so much from person to person?—and gave me hope. There is something reassuring in not knowing for sure how I will ultimately be affected.

This time, too, I noticed something that maybe explained why I'd come back: the meeting was . . . well, fun. Sure, we talked about serious topics—drugs, cures, insurance problems, wheelchairs—but we also had a good time.

I left the April meeting with a compliment on my new foot braces and a heart full of hope, and the next time I have a panic attack I'm going to think of that room full of people—those strong, courageous, kind people that I hope I'm like. Sometimes, I'm learning, you need to buy yourself a milkshake and face your fear and dread head-on, then stand back and get some perspective so that the real truth may be revealed to you.

Chapter Twenty-six

DRESSING
May 2004

I watch pregnant women. I watch them in airports, malls, grocery stores, parks, and parking lots. I watch them wistfully, thrilled at their strength and agility as they walk fast, despite their high heels, despite the bags they carry.

As my pregnancy has progressed, I've been falling even more, and my watching of pregnant women has only increased. The falling might be worse because of the physical strain pregnancy is putting on my already stressed muscles; it might be worse because my balance is off with the new twenty pounds collecting on my torso; or it might be worse because my left foot is going the way of my right foot. I'm inclined to believe it's the latter, because these recent falls are different from the falls of my past: when I get up, both my knees are skinned and later they both bruise. In the past, I would skin only my left knee because I'd trip on my right foot.

The falls stopped or slowed for awhile, thanks to my new right foot brace and more acupuncture. But now that I'm falling again, I can't help it—I'm scared. I've heard too many stories not to be, like the story a friend and her partner told me. They said that they knew it was time to move their bedroom to the first floor when my friend got out of bed one morning and fell on her face; her arms were no longer strong enough or fast enough to slow her descent. I thought of her the other day when I stood up from my second fall. I'd been climbing the stairs to the deck, and at the top one, I didn't lift my foot high enough. It got caught in the space between the stairs, and the next thing I knew I was face-down on the porch. I'd like to think I wrapped my arms around my stomach to cushion it from the fall, but I'm not sure where they were, so focused was I on my face. First the left side and then the right side of my face skimmed across the deck, knocking my glasses askew. My face hurt all afternoon; now, days later, I am still peeling off pieces of skin, and I look like I have a sunburn.

So when another friend with ALS e-mailed me to say that she had just wiped out in the dressing room at Sears—her knees and ankles just gave out and down she went—I couldn't help but think of her down on the floor like that and remember my face dive and the story of my other friend's wipeout. And then I thought of the Jelly Bean, the first person I think about whenever I fall.

* * *

In addition to studying pregnant women, I also study shoes. I study my friends' shoes and the shoes displayed in store windows. I study the feet of new mothers, too, especially the ones wearing clogs and lugging tiny baby bundles; they don't look the least bit scared that they will fall. The other night, when I was watching a documentary about a man with ALS, I studied his feet as well, mesmerized; he wore Dr. Martens with a nice thick sole. I wanted to step into the film and ask him how he did it, how he walked in those shoes.

I study my own shoes, too. I have two piles of them. One, in the attic, comprises athletic sneakers, high-heeled sandals, big and clunky clogs, and a pair of biker boots. I hope to one day wear—and walk in—these shoes again. For now, I draw from the second pile of shoes, which is on the first floor of the house: some red slides I wear in the mornings pre-bracing, a low pair of black Mary Janes, and some hard-bottomed trail shoes. If I never had to wear or see these three pairs of shoes again, I would not be unhappy.

One of the selling points of my new leg braces, my AFOs, was that they would supposedly be thin enough to wear with dress shoes, not just sneakers. So after I got them, I tried them on with my beloved Danskos. Wouldn't fit. I slid them into my clunky, high-heeled Mary Janes and they fit, but I couldn't walk with the extra inches under my feet; between the heels and the plastic brace, I felt like I was pitching forward. I knew better than to try the brace with my biker boots, summer sandals, or clogs. Finally, I spent a few hours at one of my favorite shoe stores, trying on shoes, and that's where I realized that "dress shoes" meant *men's* dress shoes. I walked out with the only pair of summer shoes I could find that would fit over the braces: some Tevas.

But even as I sputter about the braces, I can't imagine not having them. It took weeks to get the order through my insurance and make the braces; each one cost $857. Given all this, now that I have them, I guard them carefully.

So the other night, when my braces were off, and Steve picked one up and examined it, I got nervous. I trust Steve with my life, but he was handling my *brace*. I watched him and recalled a character in a Flannery O'Connor story who cares for her artificial leg like it's her soul. I've taught that story at least thirty times, and the other night, for the very first time, I understood where that character was coming from.

* * *

Now that I am committed to wearing the two braces, I check out pregnant women even more. In the waiting room at the ob-gyn's I casually scope out other women; at the movies, before the lights dim, I covertly examine a pregnant friend's attire. And one recent sunny Sunday, I ogled pregnant women on Boston's Newbury Street. "How do they look so *nice* and put together?" I asked Steve. He didn't know; he was busy checking out fancy baby strollers as if they were the newest offerings from Toyota. "We need one of *those*," he whispered to me as an Eddie Bauer one went by.

I looked down at my own outfit. That day, I was wearing a pair of low-rider cords from the Gap, size ten, that fit under my belly. Steve had put a key ring on the zipper so I could zip them up more easily, and I'd strung one of his belts through the loops. It wasn't much use: whenever I reached for something, the pants dropped lower, my shirt rode up higher, and the braces bulged funny when the pant leg moved. I felt like Mrs. Frump.

The problem is that I'm tightfisted, and I've been trying to get by with just my old clothes and two maternity pieces. But I was busting out of my old clothes, and getting dressed each day was frustrating. And it was hard to feel attractive, what with my funny, skinny body; my big, fat belly; my white, atrophied legs; the clunky braces;

and the ill-fitting clothes. I couldn't do anything about my body or the braces, but, I decided, I could do something about my wardrobe.

Pregnancy clothing, however, depressed me, and I dreaded four and a half months of wearing that attire. Indeed, it confounds me that a culture that invented Pop-Tarts and Post-it notes and Velcro can't come up with a shorter pregnancy—or at the very least better maternity clothing. Few of the maternity clothes fit me, and even fewer are attractive. If the Bush administration really wanted to stop teen pregnancy, they'd arrange to take teen girls on a tour of maternity clothing stores and departments, and show them what they'll have to wear if they get pregnant. *That* would cut down teen-pregnancy rates. I finally found a swanky maternity shop where I bought two pairs of jeans and three shirts; in two hours, I spent more money on clothes than I usually spend over the course of six months, but it was worth it. For the first time, I felt almost like a Newbury Street Pregnant Lady.

* * *

These days I try to watch only myself.

I'm trying, hard, to make peace with the leg braces and with my new body. For a while, I wore the right brace just to get used to it. One night, I wore it with a skirt, over my pantyhose, to a party. I also wore one of my new shirts, which emphasized my big belly. I was the only pregnant woman at the party, and I was also the only person with a disability. Mingling with my friends, I felt like a startling contrast, a walking dichotomy.

Only one person mentioned my brace, but several mentioned my stomach. This is the downside of my new shirts—they fit snugly, close to my stomach. All night, I dodged the hands coming for my stomach; I never knew when someone would attempt to feel me up. There had been a lot of drinking, and perhaps that loosened people's inhibitions, but I felt a bit like a moose at a Maine Hunters Alliance convention.

But for the most part, I felt attractive, despite the belly and braces. This has taken some revised thinking on my part. I used to be considered attractive; I was tall, blond (fake, but most people didn't know that), healthy, and fit.

I don't feel long, lean, and limber any more. Although I am still a fake blond and I am still tall, I am not physically the woman I used to be. I find it hard to watch people watch me walk my lopsided, awkward walk. It is hard to feel sexy or walk confidently when you teeter on legs stiff as Popsicle sticks; when your leg muscles are all but nonexistent; when hard plastic jabs your heels and sucks on your calves; and when a river of warm, plastic-induced sweat runs down your calves and under your feet, a slick layer between flesh and brace.

When I look to the outside world for confirmation that

"disabled" can be attractive, I am hard-pressed to find it. It fascinates me that so many stars have made maternity sexy; *People* magazine usually contains a pregnant star or two decked out for some party. However, it is rare to see disabled stars featured for their glamorous looks or evening gowns, or disabled models selling casual wear.

So these days my imagination gets more of a workout than my mouth (and that's pretty busy, thanks to pregnancy cravings); I fire it up again when I open a magazine at the nail salon. I pretend that the pages I flip through show a sexy-looking Britney Spears sporting an AFO, a swaggering George Clooney with a walker, a smiling Madonna with a cane and flat-heeled shoes, and a close-up of Ben Affleck signing autographs from a wheelchair. Mind you, I don't wish disability on anyone, but it is nice, for just a few minutes, to pretend that we *all* agree that a wheelchair or a brace or a cane doesn't make one less talented or less appealing. I'm trying to convince myself of this as well—that talent and beauty come in different forms, and that leg braces, an ALS body, and a pregnant belly don't render me unattractive.

Back in the fall, I read a book by a man who had ALS. In the book, he said that after getting ALS I would never again be physically comfortable, but that I could get used to—and be thankful for—being in only a *little* discomfort, and that I could learn to enjoy being "comfortable enough."[3] Between the ALS and the pregnancy, I am rarely comfortable, and some days, it is hard to remember to be thankful for being only *slightly* uncomfortable. However, there is no denying that I like being alive enough to know the difference between comfort and discomfort; that I'm grateful for my mind, which works well enough to remember what comfortable felt like; and that I'm aware of how powerfully lucky I am to gain this weight, to grow fat with this child.

Chapter Twenty-seven

LIVING
May 2004

I wake up at six to birds chirping outside the skylight above our bed. The weekend weather is supposed to be springlike, and I keep thinking of this as I try to will myself back to sleep. It's no use. I'm awake. It's a beautiful day, and I long, yearn, pine to run. I get out of bed, hoping the ALS has disappeared while I was sleeping. It hasn't.

Downstairs, I open the sliding-glass door to the deck and test the air. It smells of spring and I think of my bike in the barn. We live in a runners' and bikers' paradise, and I briefly contemplate finding my fancy biking shoes, pumping some air in the bike tires, clipping my feet in to the pedals, and going for a ride.

Instead, I go inside, make tea, and pay bills. Steve gets

up. We eat breakfast, go to the dump, and then head to the beach for a walk. Even though it looks like a good day, nothing pleases me: our breakfast options, the lines at the dump, Steve's driving—all of it annoys me.

We are halfway to the beach when Steve asks what's wrong. At first I say nothing, but then I tell him how angry I am not to be able to ride my bike or run this morning. How hard it was to pass all the bikers and runners as we drove to the dump. How excruciating it is to smell the spring air and not be able to race around. I think back to last spring, when I was just starting to get into a running routine, when I took frequent three-mile power walks at the beach, when my bike would call to me and I could answer. These days, my body considers a good workout getting the groceries or doing the laundry, taking a shower, or getting dressed.

I don't tell Steve that I am scared out of my mind by how much I've changed in a year. Instead, I blow my nose and wipe my eyes and tell him I'm ready for our walk. By the time we reach the end of Ferry Beach, Miss Crankypants is gone.

This outburst isn't unusual. On average, I spend about fifteen minutes a day feeling crabby and sorry for myself—some days more, some less. I'm finding that warm-weather weekends are the worst; these are the days I most miss my old active self and I go crazy not getting to work out. These are also days that I am out of my weekday routine of appointments, writing, and ALS work, and my mind has too much time to think. However, I see this moping time as a fairly healthy way to mourn my losses; a lot, after all, has changed in the past year. After I've had a good, productive worry, I package the emotion up and put it elsewhere so that I can enjoy the day.

And I have a lot to enjoy, to be thankful for. Most of my friends and family members understand this; for the most part, they treat me just like they used to, only with a little more forgiveness when I'm cranky. However, there are a handful of people who don't get it—who feel sorry for me. Recently a friend complained of some problems she was having, then said, "I feel so bad complaining about my life, when I look at *yours*." Her words caught me by surprise, but they shouldn't have: several people have said this to me. Of course, I would much prefer not to have ALS, but that aside, my life isn't that awful. *Look at my life,* I wanted to reply to that friend: *I have a boyfriend who cooks, gives a great back rub, and moved across the country to be with me; I have a sweet house, a baby on the way, loads of good friends and family, and time to write in the mornings. I tend not to waste time doing stuff I don't want to do anymore, I've finally become a little more assertive, and I appreciate things that the old me often took for granted.*

When I told another friend about this epiphany of mine, she agreed, then said: "You've got everything you've wanted all along, and you got it all in less than a year. You're living a fast-forward life."

A fast-forward life: that's it. I look back at the past few months, then ahead to the uncertain future, and I imagine buckling up, throwing the road map out the window, and letting the universe take me where it will. No questions. No answers. Just me, my courage, and the open road; the smell of hope and discovery in the air, and the promise of a lot of pit stops and scenic detours along the way.

Chapter Twenty-eight

HIKING
June 2004

I am standing at the bottom of the stairs that connect our first and second floors. There are thirteen steps between me and the bedroom, where I want to change my clothes. I grab the handrails and survey the situation. If I go slowly, carefully, hands on the rails, I'll be able to do it.

I meet Steve at the top. After offering his help, he says gently, "Climbing Everest?"

I nod. Smile. I am panting. In four steps I'll be at the easy chair on the landing. And I will. Sit. Down.

* * *

Everests everywhere. These days my right arm can barely lift a coffeepot, and I am slowly winnowing out our glass collection, thanks to dropping and breaking them. It's hard to hang coats up in the closet; when did they get so *heavy*? For two weeks I've been trying to get into an ALS drug trial, making phone call after phone call, only to be told yesterday that there's no such trial because there's no such cocktail. I just gave up my basic yoga class; I grew annoyed at not being able to do so many of the poses.

More Everests, like the challenge of typing, which has become excruciating as my right hand slows down. Right now, I think of each word carefully before typing it; I am eager not to waste a single hand movement. I don't bother capitalizing words or correcting spelling; I know my spell-checker will catch errors, and I will agree or disagree with it, simply by moving the mouse. E-mail is absolute torture; I get long e-mails and am tempted to delete them. How will I ever respond?

Yet even as my typing speed slows almost to a halt, the voice-typing program still sits on the bookcase near my desk, unused. I don't think there's much point in learning how to use it, because I'm losing my voice, too. Yesterday, for the first time, I lost it before evening. It started to go at lunchtime, and all afternoon I struggled to be understood. I hated how *stupid* I sounded as I slowly forced letters into sounds, and then sounds into words.

All of this. And on top of it, the deadline approaches for a speech I'm supposed to give—an *inspirational* speech. I know I wouldn't want to listen to some woman complain about how much ALS *sucks,* but I'm just not feeling very inspirational right now. I'm angry and frustrated and tired of doctors' appointments and everything ALS-related.

"The problem with ALS," I said to Steve the other night, "is that you just can't sit back and enjoy having a fast-moving, debilitating terminal illness. You have to spend all your time dealing with doctors and support services. And all I desperately want to do is find a lake I can swim in."

Instead, I spend hours talking with organizations that loan equipment or doctors' offices. But I'm quickly learning not to expect something the day you need it. *Anticipate your needs well in advance* is the unofficial bumper sticker of the ALS community, because the world does not operate on the ALS timeline. As a result, two months is the average turnaround time for anything ALS-related. Leg braces? Two months. A shower seat? Two months. An out-of-state doctor's appointment approval? Two months. Hell, I made my October wheelchair appointment back in *May.* And the machine that will talk for me if I lose my voice? I've been told to give it six months. It's hard to be optimistic about a miracle or a cure when you're making plans for an electric wheelchair, and when a walker and commode sit in your basement, waiting for you.

* * *

This morning I've been humming the song "If I Had a Million Dollars." I've wondered often what this ALS would be like if I were independently wealthy. Already I see the difference between my experience with ALS and that of people who earn less than I do. Prescribing me vitamins that may or may not help the ALS, my doctor tells me to buy them, they can't hurt, but points out that this is a luxury that not all people with ALS can afford. Swallowing the handfuls of vitamins and paying the increasing vitamin bills, I soon see why.

When, in the early days of my diagnosis, I read that ALS is the most expensive disease one can have, I didn't really believe it. I figured that my insurance would cover everything. These days, I see how quickly the numbers add up. A friend tells me her braces cost $2,400, and she paid 20 percent of it; plus she had to buy new shoes that she could wear with the braces. A woman whose husband has ALS bought a secondhand elevator; they paid for it out of pocket, so the husband could get around the house.

Then I look at my own situation: the commode, the cane, the braces, the walker, and the shower stool—all covered by my insurance. The handicap-accessible car? Not covered. The lift to take me from the driveway into the house ($9,000)? Not covered. The $2,000 in renovations we'd have to make to accommodate the lift? Not covered. A lift from the first to the second floor? Thirty-three hundred dollars. And, of course, not covered. A friend with ALS needed a computer program that "speaks" for her and doesn't require typing. Her insurance probably would have covered it, but she didn't have time to wait. She needed to communicate *right then,* so she paid for it herself.

I could see why. If I had a million dollars, I'd buy a lift and not waste time checking out loans and grants for equipment. If I had a million dollars, I'd pay for the renovations to go with the lift and I'd put in an indoor lift, too. I'd buy myself an automatic page turner so I could read books again, and I wouldn't flinch at the price (over $1,000). If I had a million dollars, I'd buy the shower seat of my choosing and have it delivered, same day. I'd give some money to research, to find a cure; and then I'd rent a cabin on a nearby Maine lake for a few summer weeks, a cabin with easy access to the water, and I'd swim every day that the weather allowed.

But I don't have a million dollars, so instead, my friends and I dream of an ALS fund that would help offset my ALS expenses. So we form Girls Kick ALS, and we meet every few weeks and plan fund-raisers. Other friends join us at events, donate their skills, or organize fund-raisers in their communities. Family members attend events, help organize and raise funds, and get the word out. These friends and family of mine donate their time, skills, and energy, despite having full and busy lives of their own. It is nothing short of amazing, what they accomplish.

A friend with ALS tells me that her friends don't like to talk about ALS. I am incredulous—then I look at my friends and family and know, once again, how lucky I am.

* * *

The closer my due date gets, the more I am shocked by the economics of babies: the emphasis on outfitting a nursery, the elaborate gift registries at stores like Baby Shopping Consumes Us, and the abundance of baby goods. Maybe it's the ALS talking, or maybe it's the old cynical me surfacing on steroids, but I refuse to turn this momentous occasion—the birth of my child—into a consumer-driven buying frenzy, and I refuse to spend the time I have left over in my day after dealing with insurance, doctors, and equipment suppliers decorating a nursery or investing in the best developmental toys.

This isn't to say I won't be grateful for any baby presents we get, because I will be. In a big way. However, it is aggravating to see what a consumer sport parenthood has become, especially when I can think of more important things to spend money on than a brand-new matching nursery set. But I know well that, were it not for the ALS, I, too, might be wandering around the nearest baby mega-store, my vision blurry, my mind focused on all things baby, checking off gift-registry items with abandon.

Chapter Twenty-nine

LOVING
June 2004

I have spent seconds, minutes, chunks of time watching an ordinary man mowing.

I have studied the way the muscles in his legs flex and move as he pushes the mower over the side lawn. I have propped myself against the fridge and watched the ease with which his feet lift as he walks, almost runs, after the machine. I have seen the sun on his strong arms, arms that can haul a pregnant woman to her feet in seconds, arms covered with a thin layer of red hair.

I have watched him the way he watches a movie after an especially draining workday, fixated, oblivious to the rest of the world. Yes, I have spent much time watching a man mow the lawn. Just an ordinary man. Mowing.

* * *

Sometimes I go into Steve's study and open the leather-covered album full of our correspondence. I read our old e-mails and am shocked that it was only a year ago that our correspondence began. At times like this, it is unbelievable to me, all that has happened since then: my ALS diagnosis, Steve's move to Maine, our new home, my pregnancy.

As we pass our first-year anniversary and move toward our second, I study Steve carefully. How does he put aside the ALS and see me as a partner, an equal, not just a diseased woman for whom he must care? How does he let himself love fully someone who has a death sentence?

And me, how do I stay as independent as possible, and yet as much a part of the relationship as I can? How do I not feel bad for all that Steve has given up to be with me? It takes constant work to not feel guilty for all that he has lost and to remember what he has gained: a partner who adores him, a child on the way, a family.

In the past few weeks, I've given two speeches and been profiled in a Maine paper. The positive feedback was thrilling and made my head swell.

Steve, however, isn't giving speeches or being interviewed or getting any accolades. He is too busy working, mowing the lawn, picking me up, reading a baby book, helping me dress, building me smaller stairs, researching ramps and lifts, escorting me to events, proofreading my essays and speeches, and picking me up again.

Some nights I watch him doze on the couch while the TV blares a movie, and I am overwhelmed by how lucky I am. I lean closer, brush my good hand over his face, run my fingers through his hair, and kiss his cheek. I look at him, and I know: he is no ordinary man.

Chapter Thirty

WALKING
July 2004

The gift of walking is wasted on so many able-bodied people.

The sentence comes to me just like that, fully formed and in an italicized print, as I sit in the lobby of L.L. Bean, waiting for Steve to pay for his fireplace tools and doormat. As I wait, I watch. ALS has made me a much more patient person, although friends and family might dispute that. Before ALS, I would not be as easily entertained as I am now, watching this lobby scene like a documentary. I focus on a pregnant woman, an employee, as she walks past me, pushing her stomach before her. Her legs are huge and swollen and I just *know*: she appreciates and feels each step those legs take.

Others, though, seem to take this gift for granted. I watch hugely overweight people struggle to the elevator. I watch young men with strong legs tool along in a leisurely fashion. I study the girls and young women in their high heels—too hobbled for more than a slow-paced stride. What a waste, I think, and I long to trade legs with them, or at least give their legs to the pregnant lady.

And I think of myself: where would I have been in this crowd a year and a half ago? I would have been walking fast, annoyed by the slow walkers. I would have been taking the stairs, eager to get in and out fast. I would not have been thinking about how very fabulous and lucky I was to have a pair of legs that worked. I didn't run my errands gratefully, knowing that my healthy, agile body was only a diagnosis away from disability. I am sure of this.

* * *

Yesterday, for the first time since last August, I tried to go swimming in a lake. We are staying at a cabin our friends have kindly lent us for the week. The hundred-year-old structure is quaint and charming and sits just feet from a large New Hampshire lake. Unfortunately, though, the coast is rocky and I cannot get in the water. It is hard, being so close to a lake yet unable to get in—sort of like being in a room where everyone else is drinking a dirty martini, yet I can't. I long to stretch my legs down over the rocky shore, balance myself with strong arms, and throw myself in for a good swim.

Fortunately, there is a sandy, accessible town beach two miles away, where, yesterday, I took off my braces and headed to the water, balancing myself on legs that much prefer to walk with braces. It was hard to walk in the shallow water, and I had left my cane on the beach, so I held on to Steve for a bit, then fell in the water.

Here was what I felt: the cold of the late-afternoon water, followed by a panic unlike other panics. My lungs are working hard these days. I've lost about 0.5 milliliters capacity since October, and the cold water knocked the wind I have left out of me. And although I appreciated the weightlessness of the water, I couldn't help but notice, as I tried to float, how little fat and how little muscle I carry. I treaded water for a while, and then I stumbled out, back to my beach chair.

* * *

Later, sitting on the screened-in cabin porch just a few feet from the water, I thought of swimming and walking and moving easily. And I cried.

But this morning, sitting on that same porch, drinking coffee, feeling a morning breeze, admiring the large expanse of water just feet from me, I think: I was in this lake yesterday. I remind myself of how fabulous I looked, in a pregnant sort of way, in my Prego two-piece jungle-print bathing suit. I feel the flutter of the Jelly Bean inside me, and I think: there is still time for a cure, a reversal of symptoms, a miracle. There is still time.

Chapter Thirty-one

COOKING
July 2004

I start making dinner at 6:20 PM. Too late, I know. It will take me forever. I'll need to open and rinse two cans of beans (ten minutes); chop garlic, onion, celery, and cilantro and sauté them with the beans (at least twenty minutes); and then mix the cornbread, my right arm permitting.

Steve is home from work and offers to make dinner. He is an excellent cook, and when we started dating, my sister, a noncook, remarked on the unfairness of it all: that two good cooks would date, thereby lessening her chances of finding a guy who cooked. I laughed at her comment then, but as my fingers and arms grow weaker, cooking becomes less of a pleasure and more of a chore, and I am grateful that Steve is so adept in the kitchen.

I have also become increasingly grateful for the wide availability of frozen and processed meals. The old me, pre-ALS and pre-pregnancy, was a picky, even snobby, eater.

These days I am an appreciative dinner guest and an even more appreciative cook. Indeed, on the few occasions when I cook or bake, I am slow, focused, methodical. Every movement is performed in slow motion. Like the night I made a dear friend a pie: it took me hours and required several rest breaks. The end result was hardly *Gourmet* quality—the crust was perfect in a store-bought kind of way and the lime slices on top were cut unevenly—but looking at it, I had a brainstorm. I should have my own TV show: *Cooking with the Disabled Chef* or *In the Kitchen with ALS*. I gazed at my pie and thought of all the episodes I could do: "Tossed Salads in Fifty Minutes or Less," "Tuna Casserole in Three Hours," or, "Beyond Aerobics: You Too Can Make a Key Lime Pie."

I tell Steve I am fine to cook by myself. "So what's the ETA on dinner?" he replies, trying to plan the length of his run. I look around the kitchen. I still have to make the salad. I decide against putting carrot in it. Too much work.

"Forty-five minutes," I say.

Steve opens the buttermilk for me and leaves for his run. When he returns, we will set the table and dish up dinner. Then we will eat. Slowly. Mindfully. Thankfully.

* * *

I wasn't always a slow, appreciative eater.

Until, that is, my junior year of college, my first year at Smith College, where I found a group of women I liked—they were funny and smart and not the least bit pretentious; in addition to hanging out together until the wee hours of morning, we also ate together.

I had eaten meals with my family around dining room tables, and for the past two years I'd eaten with friends in the cafeteria at Bates College, where I'd spent my freshman and sophomore years. I was used to eating quickly, gulping down bites before someone else ate the last of the stuffing or steak, or inhaling a quick meal before dashing off to class or work.

All that changed at Smith, thanks to one of my new friends. Watching me eat one day, she admonished me to *slow down*. Momentarily, I was embarrassed. But by the next meal, eager to fit in, I had heeded her advice.

I wish my Smith friend could see me now. Thanks to ALS, eating—wrapping my fingers around the fork, picking up a heavy piece of flatware, cutting a tough piece of lettuce, and getting food from my fork to my mouth—takes effort and concentration. I am the slowest eater I know.

I am learning to take pleasure in smaller amounts of foods. I limit my coffee intake to one cup a day. I have cut back on refined sugar. And I've become content with occasional sips of wine or beer instead of a whole glass, like the other night, when we went out for pizza and I took a small sip of Steve's porter. It was the beer I would have ordered, were I able to, and I rolled it around my mouth, enjoying the heavy surprise of it, savoring my sip as others enjoy an expensive wine.

Sometimes, when I find myself dining with fast, agile eaters, I feel a momentary flash of envy—what I would give to gulp my food down like that!—and then a weird sort of sadness for them. *Slow down*, I want to say, remembering my Smith etiquette lesson, *slow down*.

But I don't fault these fast eaters. Indeed, eating so slowly—or rather, living at a pace so slow and measured, living a life that is anchored so firmly in the now—would not be my choice if I had any say in the matter. However, I can't help but notice that life as experienced from this speed is one lovely sensation after another: the familiar squish of my mom's manicotti in my mouth, the sweetness of a grape, the greenness of the peas in a tofu scramble, the slide of a knife through zucchini. I take these details in slowly. I sip them like a good dark beer. They are all mine for the taking.

Chapter Thirty-two

HOPING
Late July 2004

I t is a strange sensation, this business of being occupied. It is rare that an hour passes during which I am not aware that a small child is inside me. After all, we have, the ultrasound technician told us, an active baby. Make that an active, big baby. We know it's a boy. I spend hours watching the movement of his head and limbs against my taut skin. Some days he butts his head up high and suddenly I feel winded. Other days he performs a sideways rollover and I grab my stomach, or he stretches out a fist or foot and I have to run to the bathroom. With every twist, every movement, I experience something like triumph that the life I helped create is so active and healthy.

I've also experienced something like terror. As the

pregnancy has progressed, most noticeably these last few weeks, I've grown weaker. This should not surprise me; after all, pregnancy takes a toll even on non-ALS moms. But even though my stomach grows larger, even though I eat lots and hardly move, I haven't gained a pound in the last two weeks. My legs, mere reminders of the muscled flesh that I once had, slap around my AFOs; my arms find even an empty coffeepot heavy; my chest works hard to breathe; and my heart and brain struggle to maintain what one self-help author calls *active hope*. I practice visualization daily, and it seems to be working; I cry less and focus more on a long, healthy future.

And almost as soon as I start my visualizations, I am surrounded by signs of active, stubborn living. Driving home from the library one day, I see what looks like litter, but it turns out to be a small turtle, inching its way along Route 77. One Sunday morning when we are tooling around Casco Bay in a friend's boat, we spot a dolphin swimming near Cushing Island. And in mid-July we share a cabin with two chipmunks. One morning when I am in the kitchen, one of them jumps from the ceiling rafters down to the microwave, and then leaps to the floor before scurrying off to the dining room and who-knows-where. One night, another, more robust chipmunk dashes from the kitchen to one of the bedrooms and dances, it seems, across the bed Steve and I almost slept in, before choosing the bedroom with a lake view.

We leave the cabin one early morning and I drop Steve off at work. At home, I open the door and hear a sound. It is a familiar sound—the *kerplunk* and then mad scurry of a chipmunk—but I tell myself I'm being silly. Paranoid. The gray squirrel scurrying around our sunporch, however, is evidence to the contrary. I chase him into the living room and he retreats to my study. For hours I stay clear of my office and wait for the trapper, a Mr. Sparks, to arrive and take my squirrel away.

So what do I make of this sudden and fascinating parade of wildlife into my life? After all, it could be coincidence, nothing more. But seeing all these active lives— the squirrel, chipmunks, turtle, dolphin—I am cheered. Did I not see dead animals, including a dead squirrel, in the days before the diagnosis? The old, cynical, practical me is tempted to say that these animal sightings are nothing, just coincidence, but this year I have learned not to close my mind off to anything, to look more carefully at every detail, to not think that anything is foolish until I am *sure* it is.

So on days when despair is more powerful than hope, I visualize rallying the forces that helped grow a healthy baby to shrink an unhealthy ALS. I remember the slow stroll of the turtle, the brave leap of the chipmunk, the lazy leap of the dolphin, and the defiant will of the squirrel. I feel the kick of the lively, strong boy inside me. And I know: *this* is what life looks like.

Chapter Thirty-three

CHANNELING
August 2004

Recently I've been channeling the elderly. Or rather, my Nana. Like her, I've developed a fondness for Pepperidge Farm Milano cookies (which she loved), a nostalgia for happy hour (which she always observed), and an obsession with getting my nails done (even when she could barely drive, she always found a way to get to the salon).

So I guess I shouldn't have been surprised by what happened to me at Wal-Mart a little over a week ago. Even though I needed only a few items, I grabbed a cart and threw my four-footed cane into the basket. As the cane hit the metal, I felt the *oh!* of recognition: that action of mine had been as natural to me as brushing my teeth.

After all, hadn't I seen Nana do it every single time we went shopping?

Nana died two summers ago, in her early eighties. She was predeceased by her husband—both he and my maternal grandfather died in the late winter/early spring of 1985. Only my maternal grandmother, Mamie, has survived, rocking through her eighties as others navigate their fifties. She's eighty-eight now, and it's unnerving to me to match that high number to someone I adore so.

It's also unnerving to see how the ALS has changed our relationship. I used to spend hours talking with her—but now holding a phone is a challenge for me, and speaking is even harder, especially at a volume she can hear. Letter writing is out of the question; my right hand is on strike, and I type this with my left hand, one slow key at a time. Even our time together has changed: my grandmother helps *me* make jam. She does laundry and goes for a walk while I sleep. She waits on me, even though I am fifty-four years younger.

The same is true of Steve's parents, both of whom are in their eighties. Steve's dad opens doors for me and pries open my can of fizzy water when I cannot. Steve's mother lugs my beach towel and helps Steve with the cleaning when we go away for a week. They are in great shape: they flew here for the week to be with us, they easily managed the stairs of our home, and they live on their own without any assistance. Steve's mom told me that they get up in the morning, take inventory of what's changed with their bodies, and then go about their day as usual.

Later, thinking about her comment, I realize that my respect for the elderly has only deepened in the last few months. If having ALS is similar to growing old really, really, really fast—well, it takes a courageous person to grow old, to wake up every morning, take inventory of the changes, and not be cranky.

I am fortunate; I am surrounded by people who are patient and helpful and kind. However, when I venture beyond my immediate world, my situation sometimes changes, and when this happens, I think I understand how the world looks to the elderly. I remember how other shoppers would treat Nana when I used to shop with her, hurrying past, pushing up close, clearly irritated at her speed, or lack thereof. Now I wonder if it irked her as much as it does me when people do it to me. I think too of my maternal grandmother, who has told me how some people treat her differently now that she is old, just as people I don't know respond to me now that I talk so slowly, thanks to the ALS. Some act like I am stupid because my words are so labored; others, after hearing me talk, respond slowly, as if they think that because I talk slowly, I think and hear slowly, too. Given this, I can only imagine the kind of treatment age, white hair, and hearing loss earn the elderly.

Clearly I have learned a lot, thanks to ALS.

But now it's time for this lesson to stop. I want this ALS to go away. I want to grow old like Nana, Mamie, and Steve's parents. I want to hike many mountains with my son. I want to partake in lots more happy hours with my buddies. I want to trade my cane in for some ski poles. I want to nurse Steve through his eventual old age.

I want to wake up some morning and be thirty-four, ache-free, mobile, and naïve enough to think I'll live forever.

Chapter Thirty-four

BIRTHING

Late December 2004

On September 12, under the bright lights at Maine Medical Center, Samuel Wakefield Stout was born. He was a big guy—eight pounds, one ounce—and none too eager to enter this world: I was induced on Thursday night, and Sam didn't make an appearance until 1:38 AM Sunday morning. Minutes later, Steve placed him in my arms.

He was—he *is*—the most beautiful baby I have ever seen.

* * *

Before I gave birth, I assumed that if you were induced you would have the baby soon afterward. How wrong I was. On Thursday night, September 9, the process began, and my friends filled my room, eager for my contractions to begin. Many of them came back on Friday, waiting for the contractions to get closer. By Saturday, only one friend remained, my family hung out in the waiting room, and still I labored. Minutes turned into hours. The shift changed. Michelle and Tina came on, and Lena left. Late Saturday afternoon, the anesthesiologist gave me the epidural. As the needle slid into my back, I remembered what a friend once said in regard to natural childbirth: "They don't give out awards for that. Have the epidural."

I had been nervous about giving birth, about having a male doctor I didn't know, about being naked in front of my friend and sister. However, by Saturday, I didn't really care. I just wanted to give birth. Besides, it felt like I was in the middle of a party: the room was always full of people.

Our hope was that I wouldn't have to have a C-section. And so I pushed and pushed and pushed. When Sam emerged, everyone—Steve, my sister, my friend, a medical student, a resident, two nurses, and a doctor—cheered, and that's when Sam started screaming.

* * *

A lot has changed in the three months since then. Sam has grown big and sturdy, and he is in the 97th percentile for height and weight. And each day he grows cuter; people are always telling us that he looks like a Gerber baby.

Since Sam's birth, I have needed assistance, and there is always someone here to help me. The benefit of this is that I am most definitely a stay-at-home mother; I am with Sam every minute of the day. The other benefit is that Sam has lots of people in his life who love him and want to be with him. He is the first grandchild in my family, and the second in Steve's. In addition, Sam is the first baby in my group of friends; he has more adoptive aunts and uncles and gets more attention than any baby I know. But perhaps the biggest benefit is that Sam has so much time with his father; Steve wakes up at night with him, changes his diaper, and picks him up when he cries.

Despite these benefits, I often long to be a "normal" mother. For me, the biggest adjustment after Sam was born was getting used to having people around to help me. I wasn't prepared for the sudden loss of my privacy. I also wasn't prepared for the rate at which my body has changed. These days my voice is almost gone, I cannot use my hands, and the muscles in my neck are growing weaker. It's weird to slowly lose my fine-motor skills, my ability to talk, and the ability to walk as Sam slowly learns to control his fingers, to smile, and to move his legs. It's weird not to take him for a walk; instead of pushing Sam in his stroller, I sit in my wheelchair, Sam sits on my lap in a Snugli, and Steve pushes us.

When I'm holding Sam, I often remember how people told me that having a child would change my life. They are—sort of—right. Having ALS changed my life. Sam is a gift, and so perfect, and so right, that it doesn't feel like he changed my life, but rather, that he was always meant to be here—and finally he showed up.

Darcy Wakefield died from ALS on December 10, 2005.

AFTERWORD

by Steve Stout

It has been four months since Darcy died, and we are falling into a new rhythm. The numbing stream of condolences has slowed to a trickle and our conversations are generally pedestrian. The handicap-accessible devices that have encrusted our home for two years are gradually finding their way to new homes. The weather is warmer and Sam can go barefoot on occasion. Darcy's mother, Nancy, stays with us four days a week and watches Sam while I work. I come home in the evenings and we chuckle over the adventures of our 19-month-old. At 8:00 each evening, I carry Sam upstairs to his room, often despite his sincere objections. But when I lay him in his crib, he is gracious if not grateful: he smiles and wraps his blankie around his face, rolls back and forth once or twice, sings a few bars of his monotonous, throaty bed song, and is asleep by the time I reach the bottom of the stairs. Nancy calls her husband and I watch a few minutes of an old movie. We retreat to our bedrooms for the night. It is newly quiet. We are inured to the unremitting bustle of our household during Darcy's last months—a house filled with the nervous energy of friends and family and hired staff— filled with the echoes of a thousand bitter humiliations— filled with anger and fear, laughter and love, and the undaunted spirit of Darcy Gammon Wakefield.

* * *

Some evenings, Nancy and I reminisce. We remember the many heartbreaking moments of Darcy's journey: her last run, her last walk, her last meal, her last words, her last breath—all ironically suffered as we celebrated her son steadily gaining the very abilities she was losing. We reassure each other that we did the best that we could for Darcy, despite our sadness, our exhaustion, and our fear. We wish that we could have been with her more perfectly—spent more time feeling what she felt—seeing what she saw. But one can only gaze into the sun for a moment. The enormity of the heartbreak she suffered, her lithe soul pinned to a wheelchair, was often too painful for us to observe. And the draining task of attending to her physical needs sometimes discouraged us from being truly present with her. We hope that she forgives us for this.

* * *

We talk about the shining moments that the illness could not take from her: her union with me, the birth of her son, the publication of her book, and the caresses of the many who loved her. We remember with astonishment the brute courage Darcy summoned to wake up each morning and not only fight ALS, but also to fight the notion that she was defined by her illness: she was, until the very end, so much more than an ALS patient. We remember the friend who would listen to the smallest of our tribulations, despite ever-present reminders that she was dying. We remember the writer who patiently made the final revisions to this book at a time when she was only able to operate a computer with the movement of her eyes. We remember the mother who fought with a determination that perhaps only mothers have to bring Sam into this world. We imagine what Darcy would think if she could see him now—awkwardly contemplating the use of silverware, walking up stairs with only begrudgingly-accepted assistance, earnestly articulating his first word, "Google," as he prances toward the computer to look at the pet-of-the-week Web site.

* * *

I see in Sam more of his mother every day. He has always had her beautiful blue-green eyes, and now her angular features are emerging as he sheds his baby fat. When I greet him each morning I see Darcy's sunlit smile. When I wonder at his energy, enthusiasm, curiosity, and determination—I remember that they are his birthright. Sam, like his mother, has a friendly word for everyone he meets. Sam likes a party—and he likes to make sure everyone knows they are invited. Sam loves to go places: he brings me his boots immediately after breakfast and very much expects me to take him somewhere he will need them. Sam has a distressing predisposition to turn the television off—even during important sporting events. He, like his mother, would rather read a book.

* * *

Sam and I spend three days each week largely on our own. These days are full. We visit friends. We walk on the beach. We read books. We eat canned green beans cleverly disguised in applesauce. We stomp around the house. We fall down. We cry. Every week, we get a little better at navigating our world—and the falls are a little less frequent and a little less painful.

NOTES

1. www.alshope.org.
2. Hiroshi Mitsumoto, M.D., and Theodore L. Munsat, M.D., *Amyotrophic Lateral Sclerosis: A Guide for Patients and Families*, second edition. (New York: Demos Press, 2001), 2.
3. Morrie Schwartz, *Morrie: In His Own Words* (New York: Dell, 2000).

Made in United States
North Haven, CT
05 October 2023

42389309R00125